"A powerful testimony of redemption, transformation, and discipleship that echoes the very heart of the gospel—life-on-life discipleship empowered by grace. Steve Trice's legacy of faith, humility, and irrational generosity has profoundly advanced our global ministry."
—*Marvin Campbell, US President, The Navigators*

"*Journey to Redemption* is more than a memoir—it's a powerful testimony of how the gospel and intentional discipleship can break generational strongholds and rewrite a legacy. Steve Trice's transparency, wisdom, and faith-filled leadership will challenge and inspire every reader. I'm deeply grateful for his life, his generosity, and this remarkable book."
—*David Meyers, President, CBMC USA*

"Steve Trice's life of raw pain, disappointment, anxiety, depression, and failure will encourage you—not only that you are not alone in your pain and struggle, but that his victory and success in life, family, and business can also be yours by following his time-tested recipe in your life—accepting the love of our Lord Jesus Christ, sincerely following the scriptural mandates of the Bible, and winning and discipling others into a relationship with Jesus Christ as spiritual reproducers."
—*Phil Downer, President, Discipleship Network of America*

"In an age when isolation, anxiety, and the relentless pressure to succeed are quietly eroding hearts and relationships, *Journey to Redemption* offers a timely and powerful message of hope. With raw honesty and spiritual insight, Dr. Steve Trice invites readers into his deeply personal story—a journey from hidden struggles to healing, from business success to spiritual legacy. More than a tribute to Jasco's accomplishments, this book is a testimony to the power of authentic discipleship, enduring faith, and

kingdom-minded generosity. You'll see yourself in these pages and will be inspired to live with greater surrender, purpose, and joy!"
—*Dr. John Fozard, President Emeritus, Mid-America Christian University*

"With disarming transparency, Steve Trice has given us a gift by sharing his story of life transformation. From hurt, anxiety, health challenges, and a life of performance to peace, joy, and well-being . . . all found in his relationship with Jesus and the power of personal discipleship. I have been challenged and encouraged by his honesty, and you will be too. A must-read!"
—*Dr. Heath A. Thomas, President, Oklahoma Baptist University; Associate Fellow, The Kirby Laing Centre for Public Theology in Cambridge, England*

"Steve Trice was a stressed, anxious business owner trying to keep up with the demands of career and family. The story of how he was transformed into a joyful man, living a purposeful life and developing a profound family and business legacy will inspire and encourage you."
—*Terry Feix, Executive Pastor, Crossings Community Church, Oklahoma City; Advisor to the Founder/Chairman, Museum of the Bible, Washington DC*

"Steve Trice has obviously spent long hours reflecting on his long journey with God and the remarkable lessons that he has learned along the way. His challenge to one-on-one relationships and a genuine walk with Jesus is a gift to any person who wants to order their chaotic life. Busy people should take a moment to reflect on what matters."
—*James Lankford, United States Senator*

Journey to Redemption

Building a Legacy of Faith, Discipleship, and Generosity

Steve Trice

Journey to Redemption: Building a Legacy of Faith, Discipleship, and Generosity
Copyright © 2025 by Legacy Stone Publishing. All rights reserved.

No portion of this book may be reproduced in any form without written permission from the publisher or author, except as permitted by US copyright law.

Hardcover ISBN: 979-8-9917432-1-1
Paperback ISBN: 979-8-9917432-2-8
Ebook ISBN: 979-8-9917432-3-5

Unless otherwise indicated, all Scripture quotations are taken from the (NASB®) New American Standard Bible®, Copyright © 1960, 1971, 1977, 1995, by The Lockman Foundation. Used by permission. All rights reserved. lockman.org

Legacy Stone Publishing
info@legacystone.com
legacystone.com

Contents

Dedication — vii

Foreword — ix

Introduction — 1

Part 1: Curse

    1. The Seeds of a Scarcity Mentality — 7

    2. The Pricelessness of Time — 15

    3. New Struggles, Old Patterns — 25

    4. The Problem with Self-Sufficiency — 35

Part 2: Power

    5. God's Model for Life Change — 45

    6. The Surprising Path of Stewardship — 62

    7. You Can't Outgive God — 76

    8. Entrusting Your Family to God — 96

Part 3: Legacy

    9. Nurturing Next-Gen Leaders — 115

    10. The Value of Life-Long Discipleship — 130

    11. Cultivating a Transformative Culture — 152

    12. Three Keys to Endurance — 164

Conclusion	174
Next Steps: Invest in Your Family's Future	177
Acknowledgments	179
About the Author	181
Endnotes	183

I dedicate this book first to my family both past and present: to my mother, Aval, who through direction and example taught me so much about addiction and disciplined recovery; to my father, Cruce, who taught me how to lead a business enterprise; to my wife, NeAnn, the love and joy of my life for fifty-three years now, who has loved and supported me through every trial; to our very gifted sons, Jason and Cameron, who are today very successful co-CEOs of the company I founded; to our daughters-in-law, Emily and Jill, and our four wonderfully bright grandchildren, Ainsley, Spencer, Landon, and Connor, who are close to completing high school and embarking on their own life journeys.

I also dedicate it to Herman Reece and Dan Williams, who gave of their time and effort to disciple and individually walk life for life with me, to help me come to know my Lord and Savior Jesus Christ, and to teach me to hear, read, study, memorize, meditate on, and apply His Word every day of my life in Him; and to the men I in turn have had the privilege of discipling individually and helping facilitate their spiritual growth for the past thirty years.

Foreword

When you live and work in the same city for more than fifty years, you begin to gain an awareness of the business leaders who share the same values as you. But, for me at least, those connections are driven less by run-ins at the golf course and more by word of mouth. Over time, I hear about leaders with a reputation for integrity, quality, and generosity, both as individuals and within their companies. Then eventually, I end up meeting those whose reputations precede them.

Maybe it's at a fundraiser where we discover we share similar interests in the causes and organizations we support. Or maybe we're introduced at a lunch with fellow business leaders, and when we finally meet, I discover that everything I've heard about the other person was true.

That's the way it was with Steve Trice. I'd long heard of Steve's business, the Jasco Products Company, before I ever met him. What I found in him was a man fully committed in his faith and equally committed to loving his family and to running a great company.

In *Journey to Redemption*, you'll find a powerful example that, when applied to your own life, can help you move from:

- a broken family to a family that thrives for generations

- a life filled with anxiety, depression, and striving to a life of peace, contentment, and joy

- a life of searching to a life of purpose, meaning, and investment.

Steve's hard-earned wisdom is helpful for every person. We are all on a similar journey of overcoming our past and finding purpose in the present. But what I appreciate most about Steve's story is his desire to point to what God has done in his life above all else. I know the last thing he wants is praise for his own actions. Rather, he wants people to see the ways—both mundane and miraculous—that God has stepped into his life and changed everything.

It's something we've always agreed on. The stories God tells are better than any stories we can tell ourselves.

I encourage you to dig deep into this book and the insights contained in its pages. As you do, I'm sure you'll find your life shifting to a new trajectory—beyond anything you can imagine. Because that's the life God the Father promises to everyone who engages in the adventure of life with Him.

David Green,
CEO & Founder of Hobby Lobby

Introduction

By all accounts, my life should be a mess.

As a child of divorced alcoholics who was sent to military school at age ten, I grew into a performance-driven entrepreneur whose drug of choice was workaholism. By my mid-thirties, I had it all, at least from an outsider's perspective—a beautiful wife, two wonderful sons, and a thriving business. But inwardly, I was deeply anxious and depressed, striving constantly for a sense of control, safety, and belonging that I could never achieve.

That all changed the day I met a man who offered to disciple me in the ways of Jesus. He pushed me to dig into God's Word, and as I've sought to obey and follow Jesus day in and day out over the past thirty-four years, I've found the peace, comfort, and fulfillment that comes from walking in a personal relationship with Him. I've learned to surrender control of my life to Him, and in that surrender, I've experienced far greater peace and freedom from anxiety.

When our sons and I first began dreaming about this book, our hope was to be able to share the history of our company, Jasco, which celebrates its fiftieth anniversary in July 2025. But the book soon morphed into so much more than that. With anything I do, my biggest hope is to spread the gospel of Jesus Christ and to introduce people to the impact of one-on-one discipleship because, together, those two things have changed my life and the lives of so many others I know. And so, as I considered how to shape this book, I realized that the best way to show the true power of those two things was to share the story of how God has utterly changed my life—and with it, the legacy of Jasco.

Though the idea of "breaking a curse" is somewhat unfamiliar to us today in Western culture, we see the effects of generational cycles every day in broken mindsets and unhealthy patterns that are modeled by one generation of a family for the next. Children of divorced parents are more likely to get divorced themselves. Addictive behaviors in parents are frequently repeated by their children. The legacies of family businesses are only rarely preserved for future generations. We may not use the word "curse" to describe those realities, but from a biblical standpoint, that is essentially what these unhealthy patterns are—the consequences of sin, resulting both from our own actions and from the sad, broken relationships and circumstances of this fallen world. Exodus 34:7b points to the truth of this when it says, "Yet He will by no means leave the guilty unpunished, visiting the iniquity of fathers on the children and on the grandchildren to the third and fourth generations."

This idea was actually quite common in the Old Testament. From the curse placed on the first man and woman after they sinned in Genesis 3, to the curses promised for disobedience to God's commands in the books of the law, to nations cursed for their rebellion against God's ways throughout the prophetic books, the Old Testament is filled with stories of people who turned away from God, tried to solve their problems in their own power, and suffered the consequences. It's a pattern we continue to see in our world today. We are born with a self-centered nature and a belief that our current life on earth is all that there is. Work is difficult and exhausting, and our relationships with our spouses, children, and friends are challenging and filled with hurt. We all have our own wounds, struggles, and lies that we've come to believe. As God's

Word tells us in Romans 6:23, "the wages of sin is death." In this case, "death" speaks not only to physical death but to death of our relationships as we go about sinning through our lives.

But as the same verse goes on to say, "the free gift of God is eternal life in Christ Jesus our Lord." In the New Testament, the story shifts dramatically when Jesus comes to Earth and takes humanity's curse upon Himself. Knowing we cannot save ourselves, He endured the punishment for our rebellion against God on the cross so that we can experience new life through the gift of faith in Him:

> For as many as are of the works of the Law are under a curse; for it is written, "Cursed is everyone who does not abide by all things written in the book of the law, to perform them"... Christ redeemed us from the curse of the Law, having become a curse for us—for it is written, "Cursed is everyone who hangs on a tree"—in order that in Christ Jesus the blessing of Abraham might come to the Gentiles, so that we would receive the promise of the Spirit through faith (Galatians 3:10, 13-14).

The curses we face in this life—the tragedies and broken relationships and struggles within our own hearts—are usually far beyond our own capabilities to fix. But through *Jesus's* power, we can be redeemed. Through His power, we can heal and even go on to live a life full of His blessings that positively impacts generations to come.

In this book, you'll read about some of the struggles of my childhood, the origin and legacy of my business, and how Jesus has changed my life through His model of discipleship. My parents each went through multiple divorces, and both died single. Addiction stole so much from my parents, my siblings, and me. Much of my dad's life revolved around his work, and while he was a great entrepreneur and business leader, the environment within the company he created was anything but Christ-like. Sadly, I've seen many of the patterns from my dad's life play out in some of my siblings' lives "to the third and fourth generations," as Exodus 34:7 predicts. I could have so easily continued down that path in my own life. My tendency toward anxiety, depression, and workaholism could have cost me my marriage and the chance to be an engaged father to my sons.

But through God's grace, at seventy-seven years old, I am on an entirely different path—one of meaning and purpose, mission and legacy.

I hope and pray that this book will display the work God has done in my life. I don't tell these stories to brag about anything I've done. I *haven't* done it. *He* has, and for that I am eternally thankful. The same redemption and life change He has achieved for me is available to you as well. My prayer is that any unhealthy patterns or curses in your life will be broken through the power of Jesus, and that your heart will be reshaped through the power of His Word. I pray you will surrender to His plan and the influence of His Holy Spirit as you learn to follow Him day by day. God is the perfect Father who longs to draw you to Himself and to transform your life—and, with it, the legacy you're leaving for others.

Like me, you may be surprised to see how He writes your story.

Part 1

Curse

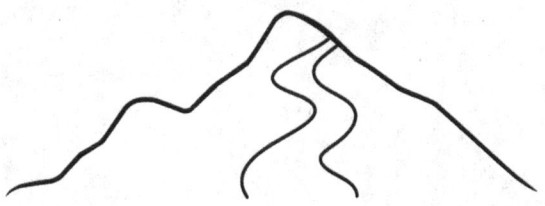

Chapter 1
The Seeds of a Scarcity Mentality

My dad was larger than life. Cruce Haskell Trice, named after the first and second governors of Oklahoma (Charles N. Haskell and Lee Cruce, respectively), was an outgoing people person. As the founder and owner of Trice Wholesale Electronics in Oklahoma City, my dad was dedicated to his company and had the highest integrity as a businessman. At work, he had a habit of approaching someone from behind, slapping the middle of their back so hard their shoulder blades almost popped together, and saying, "Let's roll it!" He worked hard to hire good people, and he always took an interest in helping his employees grow. He was loved and respected by his friends and employees alike. If you were a fellow businessperson, a University of Oklahoma football fan, or a New York Yankees baseball fan, you were probably going to be one of his best friends.

As a little boy, I counted the opportunity to hang out with my dad as one of my favorite things in the world. Though it didn't happen often, I remember going to an OU football game or two with him when I was very young, and I loved riding in the golf cart while he played a round at Twin Hills Golf and Country Club. One of my favorite memories is attending a Yankees game with my dad when I was a teenager—I even got an autographed baseball from center fielder Mickey Mantle.

One summer evening when I was eight years old, I went outside and sat on our front porch steps to wait for my dad. He had promised to pick me up after work and take me to the country club.

At first I didn't mind waiting. It was a nice summer night, and I was confident my dad would come.

But then I kept waiting.

And waiting.

And waiting some more.

By about 9 p.m., my belief that my dad would come had shifted into doubt and then a bone-deep sadness. Finally, I heard my mother step onto the porch behind me.

"Honey, you need to come on in and head to bed," she said. "Your dad's not coming."

Looking back, I don't think my dad called to let my mom know he wasn't coming. She was just very familiar with his habits by that point in their marriage. My dad and I never talked about those long hours I spent sitting on our front porch. I don't think his oversight was intentional. He carried a heavy load with Trice Wholesale Electronics, which he had founded only a year before. I'm sure he got caught up at work and entirely forgot about his promise to take me to the country club. From the time my dad quit school in the eighth grade and got his first job as a golf caddie to help support his family, he'd always been a hard worker who tended toward workaholism, and working long hours was normal for him. As I would learn, though, that meant that he almost always prioritized work over being with his family. And when he was with us, he often drank.

That summer evening, as a little boy longing to spend time with his dad, I felt his absence open a wound in my heart that would last for

THE SEEDS OF A SCARCITY MENTALITY

decades, one that would teach me to believe a lie: *All relationships will eventually be lost.*

My belief in that lie only deepened the following year when my mother sat me down at our kitchen table and told me that she and my father were getting a divorce.

"I just can't live with it anymore," she said, referring to my dad's alcoholism and his absence as a father and husband.

The second the words were out of her mouth, we both began bawling. Looking back, that was the lowest moment of my entire life.

The Devastating, Generational Impact of Divorce

For my mother, Aval Trice, the divorce marked a shift in a healthier direction. Both she and my dad drank heavily for years. My earliest childhood memory is of helping Joan, my older sister by eight years, pour booze down the toilet so that my parents wouldn't drink it and would stop screaming at each other. The thing was, it took my dad an entire bottle to pass out, but it only took my mother two drinks. It wasn't uncommon for me to come home from elementary school and find her passed out on the couch.

But a couple of years before their divorce, when I was seven, my mom joined Alcoholics Anonymous (AA), and her life totally changed—everything turned upside down and right side up for her, if you will. She realized she'd been using alcohol to anesthetize the mental and emotional pain in her life, and, coming to the end of herself, she reached out to AA for help. She stopped drinking immediately, which meant that she became a much more active and present mom for my sister and me. Though she'd always been a spiritual woman, her faith in Jesus grew as part of her involvement in AA. She also became an extremely dedicated advocate for the organization's cause. About four or five years after she got sober, she began traveling around the country speaking at AA support groups, starting every one of those speeches with the admission: "I am an alcoholic." Later, when I was a teenager, my mom frequently allowed women who were sobering up to live with us and helped them get their lives straightened out. She went from being served to being a servant, pouring herself out to help other people.

Growing up around so many recovering alcoholics, I learned that alcoholism is like climbing into a toilet and having somebody flush it. You start to go down, and if you don't reach up to grab the top and pull yourself out at just the right minute, you're dead. I was and am so thankful for the way God enabled my mother to pull herself out.

But her relationship with my dad didn't survive her sobriety.

While she had gotten sober, he wasn't interested in following suit. Whenever my dad wasn't at home, he was pursuing his business or going out drinking after work with business associates. Over time, that created a huge division between my parents. After eighteen years of marriage and spending two years trying to get my dad to consider sobriety, my mom reached her breaking point. She realized that he would probably never make the changes necessary to become a good husband and father.

According to the 2024 U.S. Census Bureau, about 43 percent of first marriages end in divorce.[1] When I consider all the children out there who are grieving the loss of their two-parent homes like I did, my main thought is this: Parents have no idea what divorce does to their children and, consequently, possibly many future generations of their families.

After my parents' divorce, I grew reclusive, spending hours on end alone in my room. I had asthma and knew how to bring on an asthma attack so I could stay home from school and watch TV. Concerned about who I might become without a man present in my life, my mother, with my father's agreement, made the drastic decision to send me away to military school.

So at only ten years old, I packed my bags and headed to Ponca Military Academy in Ponca City, Oklahoma, about one hundred miles away from our home.

Struggling with Isolation and Broken Relationships

The academy was established in 1940 by Colonel William V. Cox and his wife, Blanche, to promote the growth and advancement of young men. Located on fifty-six acres of land, the academy buildings were constructed of white stucco in a southwest Spanish architectural style.[2] By the time I arrived in 1957, the academy was home to more than one hundred boys ranging from third grade through seniors in high school.

Initially, I was excited about life in Ponca City. Going away to school with a bunch of other boys? It sounded fun. But when I arrived, I was informed that we wouldn't be allowed to call home or talk to any family members for the first thirty days. That policy was intended to break us of homesickness, but as a ten-year-old missing his home and his family, I was miserable.

Our routine as students was structured and controlled. We wore gray uniforms with black ties, shiny belt buckles, and polished shoes. We were required to make our beds with precise square corners and to have our rooms ready for inspection at any time of day. We woke up early every morning to attend classes in all the typical subjects—math, science, English, etc.—and we often went to the rifle range where we learned to shoot .22 caliber rifles.

It was a huge change for a kid used to getting to do almost anything he wanted at home. I was never a straight-A student before or after military school, but with the small class sizes at Ponca Military Academy and the rigorous discipline they taught us, I learned to be disciplined with my work and earned straight A's throughout my time there.

The culture of discipline extended to every area of our lives at the academy. For example, if we failed to polish our belt buckles or if our beds weren't made neatly enough to satisfy daily inspection, we received demerits. By the time Saturday rolled around, if we had fewer than five demerits, we were allowed to go into town. If we had more, they gave us a choice: march on the academy grounds all afternoon or go to Major Baker's office to have our demerits swatted down—five demerits per swat—with a large paddle. That meant that if we had fifty demerits, for example, we would need to take ten swats before being allowed to go into town. We could also earn "demerit slips" throughout the week by doing positive things, such as keeping our rooms clean. Each slip at the end of the week canceled out five demerits.

Almost every Saturday, I lined up behind a bunch of other guys to see Major Baker. When I walked into his office, I grabbed the arms of his chair and braced myself while he swatted my demerits down.

It sounds incredibly harsh to modern ears, and in many ways, it was. But I can't help but see value in it too. We had a choice. We didn't have to take the paddle—we could have chosen to march all afternoon. Or we could have learned greater discipline and avoided demerits altogether.

At the end of my first year in Ponca City, I was ready to be done with military school, but my mom informed me on our drive home for the summer that she was sending me back for a second year. That was the last thing I wanted to hear, and I started bawling. I spent the rest of the drive trying to talk her out of it, but she wasn't having any of my arguments. I returned to the academy for one more year.

In the years since then, I've had many people question my mother's motives for sending me to military school. I genuinely believe she was trying to do the best she could in a tough situation and that her decision was based on what she thought was best for me.

While I was in Ponca City, my dad met a pretty cigarette girl, who was a former Miss Oklahoma City, at one of the company parties he threw for his employees. (Selling cigarettes from a tray at events was a fairly common occupation for attractive young ladies in the 1950s.) Five days after the party, the woman and my dad went to New Orleans and got married. I didn't meet my new stepmother until I returned home at the end of my two years in military school, and by that time, my mom was also making plans to get remarried to a fellow AA member. My parents' second marriages, especially since they were to people I hardly knew, introduced a new loss and deepened the wound that had begun with my parents' divorce.

My dad's second marriage was a difficult one. My mother had always been extremely frugal, but his new wife enjoyed nice things and spending money. She was always urging my dad to buy bigger and better houses, which sometimes caused financial struggles. They were married for thirty years before they divorced, so there must have been something right about their relationship, but I always knew it was tough. My dad then married again, but he and his third wife divorced after only three years. My mother's second marriage was a good one—until her husband started drinking again. After that, she divorced him too and never married again. Growing up, I had example after example of broken marriages and love that didn't seem to last. My scarcity mentality grew as my fears of being rejected and losing relationships intensified.

I didn't yet have a solid faith to fall back on either. When I was young, I attended a Methodist church and later a Disciples of Christ church fairly regularly with my mom and sister. I heard good stories from the pulpit, but I didn't hear a whole lot about the Bible. I would pray sometimes, but I had no idea what it looked like to have a real relationship with Jesus Christ or what it meant to follow Him. Any understanding of or comfort from His patient, everlasting love was still far into my future.

As a result, I entered my junior high and high school years lonely and longing for connection. I was wounded and afraid, grasping for acceptance, control, and most of all, love—the kind I could trust. The kind of love that I could never lose. Unfortunately, I would go looking for that love in all the wrong places.

Chapter 2
The Pricelessness of Time

I once heard a businessman say that money is foldable time—it's what you receive in exchange for your time. You can either give people your real time or your foldable time.

"Don't think that you can give your foldable time to your family and have that be enough," he added.

As I look back on my dad's life, I can easily see how he fell into this trap. He and his second wife had three daughters, the oldest of whom was ten years younger than me. While Dad was always generous to us with his money, my sister, half-sisters, and I rarely received his personal time while we were growing up.

A prime example of this is the gift he gave me for my sixteenth birthday: a brand new 1964 navy-blue Corvette. The following year, he gave me a 1965 dark-green Corvette.

Extremely generous gifts? Yes. Above and beyond what a sixteen-year-old needs? Absolutely. Worth as much to me as time spent with him? Definitely not. Dad never withheld funds or possessions from his kids, but he withheld his time.

By the time I was in high school, all my friends knew that my family was well-off. I took my first girlfriend on dates in my fancy car at sixteen years old, which earned her the title "gold digger" from many of our classmates. Looking back, I don't recall those comments bothering me too much. I was never the most popular kid in school. Since my last name starts with T, I was always toward the end of the line for the cafeteria or anything else our class did because we so often lined up in alphabetical order. I wasn't quite last—Richard Zahn was always last—but I was way back there with him. Even though I went last and wasn't the most popular, I dated pretty girls and had a Corvette.

I probably didn't have enough respect for money as a teenager, but despite the fact that my father gave me two Corvettes, he didn't shower me with cash on a regular basis. He'd usually only give me a twenty-dollar bill when I asked for money. I also worked hard in the warehouse at Trice Wholesale Electronics in the summers to earn a small hourly wage, and thanks to my mother's extreme frugality, I learned how to stretch a dollar.

Much of the discipline I learned in military school disappeared during high school and college. I could tell you some terrible stories about my years as a teenager and young adult. I did it all wrong. In junior high and high school, I slept through algebra, and my grades dropped from A's to C's and D's. I hung out with a group of guys who drank heavily and were on the edge of trouble most of the time. When my hubcaps were stolen during my junior year of high school, I found the guy who'd taken them and stole them back. I still believed Jesus was the Son of God and that He'd died on the cross for everyone's sins because that's what I'd learned in church growing up, but I wasn't truly following Him. I didn't yet have the kind of faith that led me to make any practical changes in my life.

I chose to attend the University of Oklahoma because many of my friends were planning to go there and because *Playboy* magazine dubbed it the number-one party school in the nation. At that point, all I wanted was to get away from home and have some fun. While there, I joined a rock band as a drummer. I loved hanging out with the guys in our band, but we played at a lot of fraternity parties, and I thought the more I drank, the better I played. Looking back, the reality was probably that the more I drank, the *louder* I played. I'm paying for that now with significant hearing loss that started when I was fifty years old.

Partway through my sophomore year at OU, I considered dropping out and going to work full time. Thankfully, I decided to talk to my dad's general manager at Trice, Bob Singley, about the decision.

"Oh, no, you're not," Bob said. "Someday, you might be in a position to take over this business, and with the size it is now, an eighth-grade education like your dad's isn't going to cut it. You're going to finish school and be the first college graduate in your family. You're going back to OU, and you're getting your degree. You're going to stick with it, and you're going to study, and you're going to study hard."

Thank God for Bob Singley. I followed his advice and graduated from OU in 1970 with a bachelor of business degree with a major in business management and minors in finance and marketing.

All I can say now when I think back on my high school and college years is that I was clearly lost and wandering. All the parties, cars, and cash in the world couldn't satisfy the ache I felt inside.

Little did I know the blessing that was about to come my way.

New Hope and Continued Fears

It was a cold, foggy night in March 1971, about a year after I graduated from OU. I'd worked a long day at the parts counter at Trice Wholesale Electronics and then went to meet up with six other guys at the clubhouse of Pheasant Run apartments in Oklahoma City where I lived. The gathering was supposed to be a singles mixer. Boy howdy, a singles party? I figured it would be a great chance to meet a lot of girls.

The only problem? No girls showed up.

I still vividly remember walking over to the window, wiping off the condensation with my shirt sleeve, and peering into the darkness to see three young ladies walking through the courtyard in the general direction of the clubhouse.

"Let's go out and invite them to join us," I urged my roommate.

We did, and that was when I met NeAnn DeMunbrun, the most beautiful girl of the three.

I was immediately enamored. I worked hard to get her to sit by me on a couch as we had a drink and visited. NeAnn will tell you that we kidnapped them and brought them into the clubhouse—they weren't even planning to attend the party—but she'll also tell you, and I agree, that there was a spark between us right from the beginning. It was like we had always known each other.

Partway through the evening, my roommate punched me in the shoulder and said, "Hey, you can't have anything to do with her. She's dating the program director at the radio station where I work."

But I couldn't let that get in the way. I was head over heels and wanted to spend every spare moment with her. Before long, NeAnn decided she liked me better than her boyfriend, and we've been together ever since. Despite a few hiccups (like me forgetting her last name when I introduced her to a friend on our second date), it was love at first sight for both of us.

More important to me than her physical beauty was her heart. The way she loved her family and the way she cared for and gave herself to others was inspiring to me.

Unlike me, NeAnn had a very happy childhood. Her parents were hardworking people who loved each other and stayed together. She had two younger brothers, and her family enjoyed spending time together, whether it was going on a camping trip or doing activities together at home. NeAnn was also a person of faith. Like me, she grew up attending church, initially at First Christian Church in Watonga, Oklahoma, then later at First Christian Church in Raytown, Missouri. But her faith was deeper and stronger than mine. At seventeen, she was baptized, an experience she still considers to be a profound part of her faith journey. I hadn't attended church much during college, but I was happy to attend with her. I actually prayed to receive Christ into my heart while attending church with her one Sunday. Though I'd attended church growing up and had always believed in Jesus, I'd never prayed a prayer of salvation before. I wasn't sure I was as far along in my faith as NeAnn, but we felt like we were generally on the same page with what we believed. We agreed that if we were ever to have children, we would raise them in the church.

By the time I met her, NeAnn's dad had passed away. He was only in his early fifties at the time, his life dramatically shortened by the lasting effects of his four years as a prisoner of war in Japan during World War II. His death impacted NeAnn in significant ways, but she and her family remained close.

After a few wonderful months of taking her out to dinner, going dancing, watching football together, and visiting Lake Thunderbird with friends, I knew I was in love with NeAnn. I wanted to marry her. The question slipped out one afternoon while we were watching an OU football game on TV: "Will you marry me?"

Almost as soon as the words were out of my mouth, a terrible fear gripped me. I don't even remember her answer because suddenly I was hemming and hawing, saying that maybe I had rushed the question. The idea of marriage loomed in my mind as a terrifying and perhaps insurmountable challenge. I knew my own workaholic tendencies and feared I wouldn't be enough for NeAnn. Plus, I knew how important marriage was, how solemn and unbreakable those vows were meant to be. Yet in my own life, I'd seen them broken over and over. Would things really be any different for me?

But I had such a deep love for NeAnn. I didn't want our relationship to end in divorce like my parents' had, so I resolved to be a different sort of husband than my dad had been and a different sort of father if we ever had kids.

Two weeks after I'd originally asked her, I returned to NeAnn and made our engagement official. Marriage was still frightening in many ways, but I knew I wanted a life with her.

We were married on a snowy Saturday night, February 12, 1972, at Village United Methodist Church in Oklahoma City.

I still remember my first glimpse of NeAnn as I stood at the altar and she appeared at the end of the aisle. All I could see was her, and I was in awe. All I could think about was how I was the most blessed man on the face of the earth. And that feeling has never changed. NeAnn is the delight of my life, and for the past fifty-plus years, every two or three days I can't help but thank the Lord for sending me over to the window that night at the clubhouse so I would see her walking through the courtyard.

In the months that followed our wedding, I had the joy of getting to know NeAnn's family even better. Her brothers both got married around the same time we did, and her mother, Fran, had gotten remarried to a wonderful guy named Bob Staples. Being part of a big, beautiful family that got together for Christmas, birthdays, and other events was a pleasure. Coming from a family as fractured as mine, I hadn't even realized what I was missing.

Twelve months after we got married, NeAnn and I welcomed our first son, Jason, into the world. Two years later, we brought home our second son, Cameron.

Suddenly, I had a family—and a wonderful one at that. But although I'd found a beautiful and committed relationship with NeAnn, the fears and doubts of my childhood were still present in the background. There was a void within my heart that neither she nor my sons could fill. And it would take many years and several hard lessons to find the fulfillment I sought.

Getting My Start in Business

By this time, my career had taken a leap forward as well. I'd always hoped to work for my dad someday. When I was only five, my dad gave me my first job at Trice Wholesale Electronics: cleaning toilets and emptying trash cans. As a teenager, I worked in the warehouse helping load and unload trucks. Working at Trice was one of the main ways I stayed connected to my dad through those years, though my relationship with him was one of distant awe rather than a father-son closeness. My dad was the big boss, and I was one small cog in the business. I admired and respected him, especially as a business owner, but I didn't feel that I knew him well. Still, I was dying to work for him full time.

In 1970, that dream came true. My first full-time role at Trice was selling electronics at the parts counter, first at the downtown Oklahoma City branch and then at the main location off Lincoln Boulevard. I was promoted to purchasing agent about a year later, then to director of purchasing, and eventually to a regional manager over west and north Texas. My region included ten stores, all of which I visited every couple months, so I did a lot of driving. As you can imagine, it took a lot of time to drive all around Texas, from Pampa to Borger to Amarillo to Lubbock to Midland and then out to Hobbs, New Mexico (which was also included in my region), and finally back home.

As I mentioned before, if you were a businessperson, an OU football fan, or a Yankees fan, you were probably going to be one of my dad's best friends. Suddenly, as an OU graduate, a long-time Yankees fan, *and* a new full-time employee of Trice Wholesale Electronics, I fit into all three of those categories.

I began to get to know the part of my dad that so many of his employees had known and loved for years—the friendly, outgoing business owner who paid attention to details and did things the right way. A man who was interested in helping people grow. The entrepreneur who had built and run his company with integrity.

As an adult working at Trice, I went to OU football games with Dad almost every week during football season. As part of our work, Dad and I traveled to dozens if not hundreds of business meetings together, as well as to the Electronic Parts Show in Chicago every year. After a long day of work, I'd go into his office to have a drink and chat about upcoming decisions at the company.

My dad was the first and best business mentor I ever had. I learned more from him and the school of hard knocks than I ever did in business school at OU. After years of working closely with him, I eventually got to the point where I instinctively knew what decision my dad would make in almost any given situation. I thoroughly enjoyed that time with him, and I developed a high level of respect for him both as a person and business owner.

Unfortunately, his struggles as a dad were still quite obvious. I remember several times when I'd be sitting with him in his office around six or seven o'clock at night, and one of my half-sisters, who were all still very young at the time, would call him.

Upon answering the phone, his response was nearly always, "Honey, I'm busy right now." And then he'd hang up. *Click.*

"Dad, don't *do* that," I'd often say. "Talk to your daughter."

To this day, any time I get together for lunch with my half-sister Sherie, she'll ask me, "Steve, can you tell me a story about our dad? I didn't know him. You did."

Of course, I always do. The truth of her statement still grieves me though. I'm so grateful for the opportunity I had as an adult to get to know my dad, but in my opinion, one of his biggest struggles was knowing how to be a dad to little children. I truly believe he loved his family, but I'm not sure he knew how to be present for us. As the founder of a business myself, I know how much of his attention the business probably demanded in those early years. I'm sure he didn't feel like he had much time to spare. In addition, because my dad had dropped out of school so early to help provide for his family, I think he viewed working those long hours as a way to provide for his family and didn't realize he was actually neglecting them. I doubt anyone besides my mother confronted him on it either.

For me, despite my own growing relationship with him and my beautiful wife and two sons at home, many of those childhood wounds festered quietly in my heart. My scarcity mindset and my fear of losing those I loved were slowly developing into an outright battle with worry and anxiety.

I believe that, by nature, we all have certain sin issues we gravitate toward—things like anger, anxiety, lust, greed, and pride. My dad struggled with prioritizing work above all else, while anxiety has been my biggest struggle. The challenges of my childhood only enhanced it—watching my parents divorce, going away to military school, coming back home to new stepparents, etc. I was already anxious by nature, but those events exacerbated my natural tendencies.

While I highly valued relationships and was determined to be a different kind of husband and father than my dad had been, my tight grip on my family came with its own challenges. Anything that threatened my family made me anxious. Anything that threatened us financially made me anxious. Anything that threatened the power I had as a businessperson made me anxious. My brain always jumped to the worst-case scenario. I was a cup-half-empty person.

Those struggles would only become more pronounced when I made the decision to start my own business.

Chapter 3

New Struggles, Old Patterns

By the time I joined Trice Wholesale Electronics full time in 1970, business was booming. My dad's company had grown from one small store at 800 North Hudson in Oklahoma City to twenty-three locations throughout Oklahoma, Texas, Kansas, and New Mexico. For an eighth-grade dropout from Ardmore, Oklahoma, my dad had done incredibly well for himself.

As I mentioned in chapter 1, my dad dropped out of school to help support his family. He was one of seven children, and his family was never well-off. Dad became a caddie at a golf course in Ardmore, and he grew to love golf. He became quite good, and as a young man, he considered trying to become a professional golfer. However, since there was little to no money in professional golf at the time, Dad made a practical decision to go into the radio repair business instead. Eventually, he moved to Oklahoma City to work for a company called Miller-Jackson, a distributor of radio parts and later TV parts as well.[1] Over the next eighteen years, Dad worked his way up to become general manager at Miller-Jackson before deciding to go into business for himself in 1954.

Dad initially founded Trice Wholesale Electronics to sell parts for radios and TVs, but over time, his business grew to include selling full radios and TVs, as well as specialized electronic components for radios and radar equipment for Air Force bases. Around 1960, he also started a subdivision of Trice that sold five-year extended warranties for picture tubes inside TVs.

Early on, Dad recognized that he could beat out competitors by giving customers the opportunity to order from a local store instead of from his main location in Oklahoma City. In the days before the internet, a local store gave customers the opportunity to walk in, explain their problem to the salesperson at the parts counter, and get the exact parts they needed right away instead of guessing about what they needed and waiting for the part to arrive by mail. He began opening Trice stores in other Oklahoma cities, starting with Tulsa, then Lawton, Muskogee, and Okmulgee, and it worked—extremely well. By 1964, about ten years after Dad founded the company, he had opened twenty-three locations and had about two hundred employees. Additionally, the TV picture tube warranty program he started grew into a nationwide warranty business for TVs, stereos, and microwave ovens. That program became its own entity under the name Extended Warranty Company.

Trice wasn't an easy business to manage. The logistics of providing oversight to managers, operations, deliveries, etc., in so many locations was a sizable task, but my dad managed it with relative ease. People today can't imagine conducting business without contracts, but Dad and I used to do business on a handshake. Our word was our bond, and it worked well for us. My dad always did what he said he was going to do.

For all its success as a business, Trice Wholesale Electronics had a dark underbelly: its culture. My sons have both dubbed those years the company's *Mad Men* Days, a reference to the popular TV drama revolving around a 1960s-era ad agency in New York City. If you're picturing smoky offices, harsh language, and trips to the bar after work, you have it about right. There was a real camaraderie among those early employees.

People worked hard and enjoyed their jobs, but for a smaller group of people who were close to my dad, late-night trips to the bar were also a regular occurrence.

That probably doesn't come as a surprise given my dad's alcoholism, which he struggled with most of his life. Dad consistently smoked three to five packs of unfiltered Camels every day, so his office always smelled of smoke. He also had a wet bar in his office, and every day around five o'clock, he'd reach into his bottom left-hand desk drawer and pull out a bottle. He'd take a drink, wash it down with Coca-Cola, and then set a packet of matches on top of his Coke can to keep flies out. When he reached the bottom third of his Coke, he'd toss it out and open a new can to avoid any backwash. Multiple packs of cigarettes and multiple drinks a day, but the idea of drinking his own backwash was the thing that bothered him. The drinking would continue until seven or eight o'clock in the evening when he'd leave the office and head to a nearby bar with a bunch of his staff. I don't know if that culture was common at Trice branches outside of Oklahoma City, but it was certainly true at our main headquarters.

In the years since then, we've done a 180-degree turn as a company. Today the only thing Jasco's culture has in common with Trice Wholesale Electronics' culture is that we still hire quality business leaders who are good at their jobs. Looking back, even though Trice was a great company that did good work, its culture certainly had some problematic aspects. But at the time, as a young man just beginning to work his way up, I didn't think much of it. I'd grown up around drinking, and though I never struggled with alcohol the way my dad did, I had no problem joining him for happy hours at the bars on a regular basis.

For all its flaws, I'm grateful for the history of Trice Wholesale Electronics because without that company and my dad's generosity, I never would have been able to start Jasco.

The Birth of Jasco

During my time as a purchasing manager at Trice, I realized how many consumer electronic accessory products we were buying from importers. I had a growing interest in exploring whether we might begin to import some of our own products directly. Then suddenly, citizens band (CB) radios became popular.

These two-way radios allowed people to communicate over short distances, and in the early 1970s, truck drivers learned they could talk to each other with a CB radio on long drives. I knew instinctively that this was going to lead to a fantastic accessory business—every truck and every car could use a CB radio. And every person who bought one would need accessory parts like antennas, mounting brackets, plugs, jacks, and connectors. If we wanted to get into the CB radio accessory business and import our own products, this was the time to do it. With that realization, I created a plan: I would begin my own company as a division of Trice Wholesale Electronics and sell CB radio accessories to our twenty-three branches as well as to other consumer electronics stores.

I started the paperwork for the company in March 1975. NeAnn and I had one son at the time, Jason, so we decided to name the business the Jasco Products Company (with *Jasco* being a combination of *Jason* and *Company*). Cameron wasn't born until that July and has always given me a hard time about our company's name. "Where's Camco?" he's often asked. With the paperwork complete, I determined I needed a budget of

NEW STRUGGLES, OLD PATTERNS

$76,000 to get the company up and running. My dad gave me an open checkbook from Trice to move forward.

A business associate took me with him on a trip to Japan and introduced me to a trading company there. The resulting partnership allowed us to begin buying CB radio accessories and antennas directly from their factories. I hired three employees to package the accessories when they arrived and paid an outside company to create all our marketing and branding materials. Once the packaging was complete, Trice would distribute the products.

Our first shipment went out on July 15, 1975, which we deemed the official start of Jasco, our new division of Trice Wholesale Electronics.

Things proceeded smoothly for the next several months, but then in early 1976, Dad called me into his office.

"Son, you remember the $76,000 budget you brought me last year?"

I nodded. "Yes."

"Do you have any idea how much your division owes today?"

"Well," I said. "I know it's more than $76,000."

"It's a little over half a million," Dad said.

I had known the number was going to be large, but I hadn't realized it was *that* large. As always, Dad was generous with his money and gave me all the time I needed to reduce my debt to him and Trice, but the warning was clear.

I'm incredibly grateful for the flexibility he allowed me. About 50 percent of businesses fail within the first five years, usually because of a lack of capital.[2] Jasco had a serious lack of capital, and I'm certain that if we had been dependent on a bank during those early years, we would have gone bankrupt. Not to mention my anxiety would have gone through the roof. Borrowing from my dad wasn't nearly as stressful as bank borrowing would be in Jasco's later years. Because of my dad and his company, Jasco had the time and money it needed to grow and become successful. I firmly believe Jasco would not exist today if it had not been for Cruce Trice and Trice Wholesale Electronics.

In 1977, I bought Jasco from Trice, and by 1982, we had paid our debt back with interest. But no success comes without cost.

Growth Pains

Those first five years of Jasco's history brought both amazing opportunities and daunting challenges. In March 1976, I dressed up in my red leisure suit with a stars and stripes tie—high fashion in the '70s—and went to the Personal Communications trade show in Las Vegas, Nevada, to display Jasco's products. During that show, a gentleman named John Grable walked up to our booth and handed me his card. Glancing at the card, I saw that he represented Target stores.

My pulse leapt. Was there a chance Jasco could begin selling to Target?

"I like your products. I'll be in touch," Mr. Grable said.

When I didn't hear from him after the show, I began calling. Over the next few months, I called him five times, leaving messages every time, but I never heard back.

Finally, in October of the same year, he called. "I really liked your products at the show," he said. "Would you like to sell them to Target?"

"*Absolutely*," I said.

"Well, why don't you get on a plane and come to Minneapolis, and we'll see if we can work out a deal."

Little did I know then how big a part Target would play in Jasco's growth as a company—but that part of the story comes later.

One of the biggest challenges for me in those early years was that, in 1979, Dad decided to semi-retire and offered me the chance to become

CEO of Trice Wholesale Electronics in addition to continuing my role as CEO of Jasco. I accepted, but both companies were growing rapidly at the time, and I soon found myself overwhelmed by the responsibility.

Thankfully, about a year later, Dad changed his mind.

"Son," he said, "Ronald Reagan is seventy years old, and he's now president of our country. I'm seventy years old, and I want to be CEO of Trice again. I hope you don't mind, but I'd like my job back."

"Not only do I not mind, but thank you so much," I said immediately. "It's all I can do to take care of Jasco."

My dad took over management of Trice again but eventually sold it three years later. Three years after the sale, the new owners filed for bankruptcy and closed the company. Thankfully, since Jasco was a separate entity, it wasn't affected, other than the loss of its sales volume to Trice.

Even with the burden of running Trice Wholesale Electronics lifted, I was running myself ragged. We had gained Walmart's business by this time too, and between that and Target and the importing side of our business, I was traveling to Bentonville, Arkansas (Walmart); Minneapolis, Minnesota (Target); and Japan regularly. I had a CFO, but I was running sales, marketing, and product development. And although business was good, we had a fair amount of highly leveraged debt, along with staggering 18 percent interest rates at that time. Because of the scarcity mentality I'd developed as a child, I had an ever-present fear that whatever success we had as a company would never be enough. Any bump in the road felt monumental, and I was afraid we could lose everything at any moment.

All those factors made my job extremely challenging—and also made it extremely easy to be a workaholic. While workaholism might have made my bottom line look good, unbeknownst to me, it was taking a serious toll on my marriage and family.

Breaking the Pattern of Putting Work over Family

Before NeAnn and I got married, I warned her about my workaholic habits.

"Honey, you don't want to marry me," I told her one night. "I go to work at seven o'clock in the morning, and I don't get home until close to midnight. That's my life. It's who I am, and getting married isn't going to change that."

I'll never forget her response.

"Steve, that's all I need," she said. "Just to have you for that amount of time will be enough."

And for a few years after we got married, it seemed she had been right. NeAnn took care of the boys and managed our home life, and she never complained about my long hours. Frankly, with two young sons at home, I should have remembered the little boy I'd been sitting on the front porch waiting for my dad to come home, but that thought never crossed my mind. I loved my family, but with Jasco just starting up, I felt that the business had to take priority. And no one had yet challenged me to think differently about that. My dad had even told me once that business comes first, family second, and everything else comes after that—and as I've already said, my dad was my first and best mentor in business. I took that message to heart.

But at home, NeAnn was the one bearing the brunt of the burden, providing for our two little boys' every need and having them constantly wrapped around her legs. About two years after the start of Jasco, she finally said she'd had enough of my extensive traveling and long hours at both Trice and Jasco.

NEW STRUGGLES, OLD PATTERNS

"Steve, this is not working," she told me one day. "You're gone all the time. I'm raising our two children by myself, and it's got to stop."

I felt like I'd been hit over the head with a two-by-four.

"Wait a minute," I said. "What about what you said before we got married, when I warned you about my schedule and you said—"

"Guess what?" she broke in. "I'm changing the rules. We have two sons now, and I need you to be part of their lives."

NeAnn was absolutely serious about things needing to change. She never threatened divorce, but she didn't have to. Fear struck deep. I *could not* let what had happened to my parents happen to us. I had been so hurt, so wounded by my parents' divorce—I still was, in many ways. I didn't want that for my marriage or for our boys. But if I was going to break the patterns I'd seen in my parents' marriage and my dad's workaholic tendencies, I knew my work habits needed to change. My family needed to come first.

So that day, I stopped working such long hours. With some trepidation, I told my dad that, from now on, I was going to work only until five or six o'clock in the evening before heading home.

"Oh, okay," he replied. "Sounds good to me."

His casual response caught me by surprise, given his past advice and his own intense dedication to his job, but I was grateful for the freedom to spend more time with my family. I began working from eight to five and then went home to be with my family. In making that change, I learned that I could finish everything that needed to be done within eight hours a day, five days a week. All I'd been doing before was stretching my workload out. I still worked Saturdays for a while, but soon NeAnn reformed me of that as well.

One Friday afternoon, she informed me, "By the way, I got that job with Hallmark, and I'm going to work for them."

"Oh, terrific," I replied, trying to remember what she'd told me about the job.

"I start tomorrow," she said.

"Tomorrow? But tomorrow is Saturday. What about the boys?"

"Steve, I've taken care of them for the last ten years on Saturday. It's your turn."

That was the last Saturday I ever worked. From then on, I spent Saturdays taking Jason and Cameron to soccer games, attending YMCA overnight weekend events with them, leading Webelos when they joined Boy Scouts, and heading to the lake to fish, go boating, and camp out. NeAnn and I became teammates in parenting from that point on. Getting to be involved in my sons' lives on a day-to-day basis was one of the best things that ever happened to me, and I give all the credit to NeAnn for holding me accountable and teaching me what I doubt I ever would have learned on my own: Family is a far greater gift than any success in business ever will be.

After those two conversations, my family life was back on track, and business at Jasco continued to go well. I had my dad to thank for getting Jasco off the ground, but I was beginning to chart a different path than the one he'd taken with his business and his family. While I could tell the changes I'd made—largely thanks to NeAnn—were for the better, anxiety still loomed large inside my heart and mind. The wounds and lies from childhood were beginning to take a toll. But a series of losses and a serious health diagnosis would soon launch me into a new search for hope and meaning.

Chapter 4

The Problem with Self-Sufficiency

Dr. Richard Edwards was a man who seemed to have it all: a wonderful wife, two sons, and a thriving chiropractic practice in Edmond, Oklahoma, where he generously treated firefighters, police officers, pastors, and their families for free. He loved traveling and hunting big game, and he loved Jesus. As one of Rich's patients, I still remember the pleasant Christian music that always played in his clinic, and the light and warmth that seemed to radiate from him when he entered the room. Rich was always kind, energetic, smiling, helpful, and encouraging. It was obvious to me that he loved his work and loved using his hands to help people.

So when I stumbled across his obituary in 2015 and learned he had committed suicide, it stopped me in my tracks. *How could this happen?*

Rich's life changed forever while on a hunting trip in February 2006. A spark from his SUV's catalytic converter caught a dry hillside on fire, and before he knew it, Rich's car went up in flames. He tried to open his door, but he discovered that the locks had already clicked shut, trapping him inside.

Eventually, Rich escaped the burning vehicle and managed to make it to his hunting cabin a mile away as the fire blazed on, consuming more than twenty acres. One of his friends was at the cabin, and he rushed

Rich to the hospital. Rich would later credit angels for saving him that day, pointing to burn spots on his back that looked like wings.

While Rich's survival was miraculous, he suffered burns on more than 30 percent of his body. His face and hair were badly burned, but the worst injuries were to his hands, which were severely deformed from the fire.

In August 2010, Rich became the third person in the US to receive a double-hand transplant.[1] His family testified to his gratitude for those new hands and how he viewed them as an amazing blessing. But even with the transplant, Rich never regained full use of his hands. He sold his clinic in 2012. After that, he sank into a deep depression and eventually committed suicide at the age of 60.

By that time, I had lost contact with Rich, though I still used a vitamin regimen and several exercises he'd recommended to me, which helped me immensely with my bad back. I woke up one morning and opened the newspaper, and there was his obituary. At the time, I was attending a church of about eight thousand people, and I'd heard once that Rich had also been a member there.

After his death, I reached out to his wife, Cindy, and asked if Rich had been in a small group at church or whether any close friends had asked him the difficult questions of life, such as if he was depressed or had considered suicide.

"Oh yes, he was in a small group," she told me. "Very regular attendance. But no one ever asked him the hard questions."

Her words hit home. Having experienced both small groups and one-on-one discipling relationships by that point in my life, I knew how much deeper you could go one-on-one. Why had I never reached out to Rich after hearing about his accident years earlier? Why hadn't I taken the initiative to see if anyone was walking with him through the real issues of life? I wished that Rich had been able to experience that kind of deeper friendship with another man, giving him a better opportunity to share openly and honestly about his pain.

Rich's tragic death confirmed my belief in the importance of one-on-one discipling relationships (more on that in the next chapter) and inspired me to begin writing a small booklet to share that message more broadly. This booklet was eventually published and distributed through the Discipleship Network of America (DNA).[2]

As I wrote in the booklet, I've learned that the hard questions are rarely asked—much less answered honestly—in group settings. In a group, men don't get asked, "How is such-and-such situation affecting you emotionally?" or "How are you coping?" or "Are you having any thoughts about suicide?" The only place people feel safe asking and answering those questions is in a close one-on-one relationship. But we've become so isolated in our culture that most people don't have that kind of spiritually related connection with anyone.

Rich wasn't someone who looked isolated. From the outside, he appeared to be well-connected with caring people. He was part of a small group, and he had plenty of friends and a loving family. But very few people knew the depths of what was going on inside his heart and mind.

The Dangers of Masking Internal Struggles

Rich died when I was in my late sixties, after I'd come to my own crisis point and experienced a dramatic shift that changed my life. But when I heard his story, I saw how clearly my life mirrored his when I was in my twenties and thirties. I had my wonderful wife, two amazing sons, and a thriving business, but internally, I was in deep pain. Jasco was growing significantly, and I was stretched thin, frequently traveling around the

US and to Asia to meet with major customers and suppliers. We were highly leveraged and changed banks a few times during those years. Every time something went wrong with the company, it sent me into a tailspin. Something as minor as an upset customer would cause me to picture the worst. In my mind, we were always on the edge of bankruptcy.

In those years, the '70s and into the '80s, my anxiety had tipped into depression. I was severely depressed to the point I had trouble functioning mentally four out of every seven days. I was so desperate for relief from the pain of that depression that it even led me to consider suicide. I never attempted it, but I thought a lot about it during that time.

According to the Centers for Disease Control and Prevention, although men make up 50 percent of the population, they account for nearly 80 percent of all suicides.[3] Many theories exist as to why suicide rates are so high for men, but commonly cited reasons include that men are less likely than women to reach out for help, and there is a stigma both surrounding men expressing emotion and around men's mental health in general.[4]

This certainly proved true in my life. Every morning, I would walk into Jasco's office, and somebody would ask, "Steve, how are you today?"

"*FAN*-tas-tic," I would reply.

And every time I would know, deep inside, that I'd just lied. But at the time, I assumed anxiety made me weak, and I didn't want anyone to think I was weak. I wanted them to see me as strong and capable. I think that's true for many men—they want to be thought of as powerful and tough. They want people to think they have it all together, whether they do or not. I know that was true for me during those years. I was so good at faking a cheerful attitude that no one in my life knew how much I was hurting. NeAnn is the only one I talked to about it, but I don't think she ever grasped the depths of my struggles, and I didn't know how to explain it to her. She had no idea what was really going on in my heart—not because she didn't ask, but because I was so good at putting a positive spin on everything. Here's how she describes that time in our lives in her own words:

> Steve has always been a positive person, and he used to say that anytime anybody would ask him how he was, he was always "*FAN*-tas-tic." I didn't know until much later that he really wasn't *FAN*-tas-tic. He was dealing with a lot of depression and stress—a lot of stuff was going on that I wasn't even aware of. When I found out the extent of his depression years later, that was a real revelation to me. He covered it up very well.

Though I was good at hiding it, a fire was burning on the inside that threatened to destroy me. Isolation was consuming me. I was alone because no one was asking—or even knew to ask—about the struggles I'd buried deep inside.

A Death Sentence

To make things worse, I lost both my parents during this time. My beautiful mother was diagnosed with mouth cancer in 1978. Although she had quit drinking decades before, she never quit smoking, and the destructive habit finally caught up with her. Over the next seven years, she had seven surgeries to remove the cancer. It seemed it was always the "next treatment" that would be the key. Time after time, we were told that the next surgery or the next round of radiation would surely cure her. During one of those surgeries, her right jawbone was removed, leaving her face sunken on that side. Another surgery removed the palate from the roof of her mouth. Each surgery was paired with radiation treatments. Finally, the doctors told her the cancer had spread to her throat. Surgery wouldn't do anything to treat it, so she would need to have chemotherapy.

By that point, my mother was exhausted and discouraged.

"No more," she said.

"But Mom, they can probably cure it this time," I protested.

I'll never forget her stone-like expression when she turned my way.

"No way," she said. "I'm done."

And she was. After that, she pretty much quit eating. She died on June 26, 1985, at seventy-one years old.

For years after her death, every time I saw a woman smoking, I was tempted to show her a picture of my mother—who had been beautiful all her life until cancer struck—and explain what smoking had cost her.

Mom's illness was tough enough, but the year before she died, my dad was diagnosed with lung cancer.

I still remember the lung specialist's words to him: "Mr. Trice, you have a grapefruit-sized tumor on your lung. It's inoperable, and it will eventually take your life."

After the appointment, I got in the car with my dad. He pulled a pack of Camel cigarettes from his pocket and tossed them on the floor of the car.

"I'm done with those things," he said.

But I knew how hard—if not impossible—that would be for him. He had smoked multiple packs of Camels a day for fifty years.

"Dad, don't do that to yourself," I told him. "Enjoy your cigarettes as long as you have to live."

As far as I know, though, he quit smoking that day. But slowly and surely, his energy decreased, and he began spending more time in bed. He passed away in May 1987.

My uncle also died of a smoking-related cancer during this time, as did several other friends of mine. In fact, between the ages of thirty-five and thirty-nine, I lost nine family members and close friends to smoking-related cancers.

Loss upon loss built up, adding to my depression and my already-fierce fear of losing those I loved. I came to view a cancer diagnosis as a death sentence. I felt that any treatments were unlikely to work because—as it had been with my mom—it was always the *next* round of chemotherapy, the *next* radiation treatment, the *next* surgery that was going to work and finally take care of the cancer. But it never did.

I was determined to stay healthy. I never smoked, I only drank in moderation, I ate the right foods, and I worked out as often as possible. Cancer wasn't going to get me like it had gotten so many people I loved.

But in 1987, the same year cancer took my dad, I went in for a routine physical as I was preparing to go on a hiking trip with my son Cameron. At the appointment, my internal medicine specialist saw something concerning in my urine sample. He sent me to a urologist for further evaluation.

The urologist delivered the bad news: "You have bladder cancer."

The word *cancer* instantly devastated me. I was only thirty-nine. I envisioned the worst, my anxiety spiking as the pain of losing so many loved ones to cancer compounded in my mind.

"It's very treatable," the doctor went on. "We'll need to do a surgery to remove it . . ."

My anxiety was steadily increasing, but I followed his advice. They surgically removed the cancer, and it didn't seem to be a tremendously big deal. I was ready to breathe a sigh of relief, but then I went back to the urologist for my follow-up appointment.

"Everything went well," he said. "We think we got everything, and I don't think it will be a problem in the future."

But as I left, he handed me a brochure detailing the type of cancer I'd had. As I read, one line stood out to me: The cancer had a very good chance of recurrence, and I only had a 50 percent chance of still being alive in five years.

I had always been a glass-half-empty kind of person, and as I looked at the glass that day, there was a big, black hole in the bottom of it. With my experience, my scarcity mentality, and my anxiety, I knew with certainty in that moment that I was going to die soon. I was going to lose my wife, my children, my career, and the "American dream" that I was living.

I will always remember driving back to my office after that doctor's appointment and praying, "If you're even there, God, this is not fair. I've got a beautiful wife, I've got two wonderful sons, I've got a thriving business. I'm not even forty, and now I'm going to die."

I was angry, *so* angry, at a God I didn't even really know. But still, one quiet plea rose from my lips.

"Lord . . . please help me."

Part 2

Power

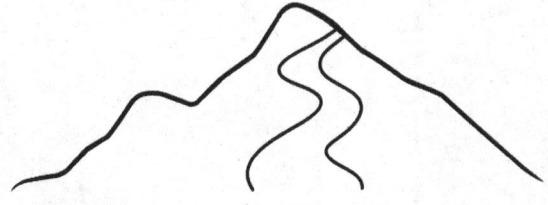

Chapter 5

God's Model for Life Change

For many people, a cancer diagnosis is the impetus they need to live life to the fullest, to pursue their dreams, or to search for new meaning and purpose in life. A quick search of headlines from the past couple of years reveals stories about cancer patients or cancer survivors fulfilling their dreams of photographing the British royal family,[1] hiking Mount Everest,[2] setting sail on a twenty-thousand-mile journey through the Northwest Passage,[3] and even going to space.[4]

My cancer diagnosis pushed me to make a change. I couldn't live with the high levels of anxiety and depression I'd been dealing with anymore, especially not if I only had five years to live. I needed to know if there was any purpose or meaning behind my (possibly very short) existence. Why had I been put on earth? What was life all about? Was there any hope for my struggles? Whether the answers came from Christianity or philosophy, I was desperate to find a solution for my internal struggles.

For the next four years, I was willing to try anything and everything I thought might provide an answer to my questions. I attended a seminar where a philosopher taught about the purpose of life, but I quickly realized philosophy wasn't going to provide what I was looking for. I went to a psychiatrist and told him about the anxiety and depression I'd been experiencing. He prescribed a drug to help with my depression, but all it seemed to do was make me thirsty.

I went to two different evangelical churches, walked down to the altar in response to the pastor's invitation, and prayed the prayer of salvation. The message from the pulpit was always that if I confessed with my mouth that Jesus was Lord and believed in my heart that God had raised Him from the dead as Romans 10:9 said, I would be saved. I wanted to be sure I was going to heaven if I died, but I was also hoping that somehow, this time, saying that prayer might help with my depression. Every time, though, I felt little reassurance in my salvation and little to no change in my internal struggles.

At one of those churches, I met with the pastor who told me I should attend their 101 class for new Christians. I did as he suggested and eventually went to their 201 and 301 classes as well, which focused on teaching attendees how to live life as a Christian, at least in a classroom-discussion kind of way. Although each of those classes was a great academic experience, Christianity never became personal for me. Nothing about my life changed, and I was left still searching, still longing for that sense of purpose and meaning.

As I look back now, I think part of my problem was that I was praying a prayer Jesus never instructed us to pray. In the Gospels, instead of asking people to pray to receive Him into their hearts, Jesus issued an invitation: "Follow me."[5] Belief in Jesus had never been my problem—I'd believed He died on the cross for us since I was a kid—but I didn't truly know Him, let alone how to follow Him. No one had ever shown me how.

In retrospect, I see God's hand on my life even in the midst of my confusion and seemingly fruitless searching. I was so desperate during that time, pushed to the very brink with despair. The words of Psalm 32:4 would later ring true for me regarding this period: "For day and night Your hand was heavy upon me; my vitality was drained away as with the fever heat of summer. *Selah*."

I felt the Lord's heavy hand on me in that season, but even though I didn't know it at the time, His purpose was to bring me to a place of hope. As Psalm 32:5 goes on to say, "I acknowledged my sin to You, and my iniquity I did not hide; I said, 'I will confess my transgressions to the Lord'; and You forgave the guilt of my sin. *Selah*."

Or, as Psalm 40:1-3 puts it: "I waited patiently for the Lord; and He inclined to me and heard my cry. He brought me up out of the pit of destruction, out of the miry clay, and He set my feet upon a rock making my footsteps firm. He put a new song in my mouth, a song of praise to our God; many will see and fear and will trust in the Lord."

The Lord was working even then to rescue me. He wasn't bothered by my despair, because He knew what the ultimate outcome would be. He just needed me to reach the end of myself before I could start moving in the new direction He had planned for me.

The Day That Changed My Life

"Would you like to come with me to the prayer breakfast that CBMC is putting on?" my father-in-law, Bob Staples, asked.

I hadn't heard of CBMC (Christian Business Men's Connection) before, but it sounded like a good chance to meet other businessmen and to spend some time with my father-in-law, a man I respected.

"Sure," I said.

The prayer breakfast was held in the basement of a convention center early in the morning on April 17, 1991. It's a date I'll always remember because it changed my life forever.

At the breakfast, Bob Vernon, the assistant chief of police for Los Angeles County at the time, shared the gospel with us.

"I used to always invite the Lord to ride with me when I was out on patrol," he said. "But then I learned that the Lord didn't want to ride with me—He wanted to drive the car."

Bob was a great speaker, and his presentation touched me, so when he invited anyone in the crowd who was interested to pray the prayer of salvation with him, I did. Since I'd already said that prayer numerous times in the past, I didn't really expect anything to change. But when they passed out information cards after the event, I went ahead and checked the box saying I'd prayed to receive Christ at the breakfast.

About two hours later, as I was working in my office at Jasco, my assistant knocked on my door.

"There are two men here to see you," she said. "One is a judge from England, and the other is a doctor from Oklahoma City. They said they just had breakfast with you this morning."

I laughed. "Sure, with me and fifteen hundred of their best friends." I figured they wanted to ask me to donate to CBMC, and I pictured telling the story later to family and friends about how a doctor from Oklahoma City and a judge from England had come to visit me. The chance was too good to pass up.

"Go ahead and send them in," I said.

The two men came in and introduced themselves. Ted Hubbard, the judge from England, sat down in the chair across from my desk. Later, I would learn that he began praying for me as soon as they entered my office. The other man, Dr. Herman Reece, was a distinguished gray-haired gentleman who shared that he was a maxillofacial surgeon from our area. Within about five minutes, he had situated himself on my side of the desk and was walking me through "Steps to Peace with God," a small booklet produced by the Billy Graham Evangelistic Association that's often used to present the gospel.

The booklet helped confirm that I did understand and believe the gospel. That had never really been a problem for me—I just doubted that believing would make a tangible difference in my life. Nevertheless, I deeply appreciated Herman's care and the kind way he walked me through his presentation.

As we were wrapping up, he asked if I would begin meeting with him every week so he could help me grow as I learned to walk out my faith.

Still overwhelmed at work, I tried to be polite in my refusal. "Dr. Reece, I'm really busy. I just don't have time for one more meeting."

"What about next Wednesday morning at 6:30 a.m.?" Herman asked.

He had me trapped. "Well, I don't have an excuse for 6:30 a.m. next Wednesday."

"Good," he said. "I'll be here in your office at that time next week."

True to his word, Herman showed up promptly at 6:30 a.m. the following Wednesday—and the Wednesday after that and the Wednesday after that.

We usually spent the first twenty minutes talking about our lives and sharing what was going on at the time. Then, we prayed together. After that, Herman would have me quote the Scripture verse he'd asked me to memorize the week before, and he would share his own memory verse in turn. We would go through an accountability chart that Herman helped me create. The chart listed the things I wanted him to ask me about: whether I'd been doing my daily quiet times like he recommended, if I was memorizing Scripture and studying the Bible, if I was sharing the gospel with others, how I was doing with my primary sin issues, and how well I was keeping up with my physical activities like working out, riding my bike, lifting weights, etc. Then we would study the Bible together, sharing our individual thoughts, reflections and personal applications.

I loved getting to know Herman and his wife, Marita, over the next few years. NeAnn and I enjoyed having dinner with them occasionally, and a couple of times, Marita baked a fantastic German chocolate cake for my birthday. They were an amazing, godly couple with a beautiful marriage and wonderful family, and they provided a great example for me in my relationships with NeAnn and our sons. From Herman, I learned the importance and beauty of humility. Such a skilled and busy surgeon taking time out of his week to meet with me, a complete beginner in the ways of Jesus, stunned and honored me.

Fairly early on in our meetings together, he asked me, "Do you think you're going to heaven?"

"Well, yes, I think so," I responded.

"Why do you think you are?"

"Well, you know, I've done everything I can to be a good person," I said. "I think I'm a good person, and I think God will take me."

"Do you know what Scripture says about that?"

"I guess I'm not sure," I said.

Herman then quoted Ephesians 2:8-9: "For by grace you have been saved through faith; and that not of yourselves, it is the gift of God; not as a result of works, so that no one may boast."

I swallowed hard. Relying on God's grace instead of my performance sounded tough, but it was a lesson I knew I needed to learn.

Time with Herman was like that. He was wise, and he knew more Scripture by heart than almost anyone I'd ever met. Through him, I was learning how to live in a new way, surrendering my heart and actions to God's will and obeying His commands as laid out in Scripture.

After a few months of meeting with Herman, I noticed a miraculous change happening slowly, but ever so steadily, within my heart. My enthusiasm for my faith was growing. I had a deepening love for Jesus and an increasing eagerness to spend time in Scripture, especially as Herman taught me how to hear, read, study, memorize, meditate on, and apply God's Word to my life.[6] For the first time, I was beginning to have a real relationship with Jesus and truly follow Him through His Word, not just have head knowledge about Him.

Most importantly and miraculously, the amount of time I struggled with anxiety and depression was beginning to lessen. The isolation I'd felt for years and the sense that no one really understood me faded away as my friendship with Herman developed and as I learned to be more honest about what was really going on inside my heart. Herman *did* know and understand what I was struggling with, and he was honest with me about his own struggles as well. It's amazing how having even one truly honest and open relationship has a huge impact on our mental health because it lets us know we're not alone.

My mindset was also being shaped by the Scriptures we studied together every week. Herman taught me Philippians 4:6-7 (which is my life verse today): "Be anxious for nothing, but in everything by prayer and supplication with thanksgiving let your requests be made known to God. And the peace of God, which surpasses all comprehension, will guard your hearts and your minds in Christ Jesus." Those verses helped me learn to thank God for every single circumstance in my life—the good, the bad, and the ugly.

The truth of Scripture gave me a new lens through which to view my past. God knew my parents would get a divorce. He knew I would be sent to military school. He knew the fears I would develop and the struggles I would have as a result. But as I looked back, I could see the tapestry God had begun to weave in my life, even then. My parents' divorce was utterly painful, but through that pain, it might be possible for me to speak truth and comfort into the pain of others, as 2 Corinthians 1:3-4 says: "Blessed be the God and Father of our Lord Jesus Christ, the Father of mercies and God of all comfort, who comforts us in all our affliction so that we will be able to comfort those who are in any affliction with the comfort with which we ourselves are comforted by God." In a similar fashion, military school was lonely and challenging, but the excellent discipline I learned there had served me well for decades as a business owner.

I began to take great comfort in my growing understanding that God was present in every detail of my life, no matter how painful. Psalm 139:16 says, "Your eyes have seen my unformed substance; and in Your book were all written the days that were ordained for me, when as yet there was not one of them." And in the New Testament, Paul writes, "Just as He chose us in Him before the foundation of the world, that we would be holy and blameless before Him. In love He predestined us to adoption as sons through Jesus Christ to Himself, according to the kind intention of His will" (Ephesians 1:4-5).

Before the creation of the world, God saw us, He chose us, and He planned to work through every single one of the difficult things in our lives to teach us how to live according to His will and to draw us closer to Him. I learned that I could thank God and rejoice, as Philippians 4:6-7 says, because He was using everything, even the difficult challenges of my life, to grow me. As I began to let go of my need for control and surrender to Him each and every day, I became less focused on my fear of losing those I loved or of losing my own life, and instead a greater peace and contentment began to fill me.

My anxiety wasn't completely gone, but I was beginning to taste a freedom I'd never known before. Similar in many ways to the help my mother found through the accountability of AA, I was experiencing the transformative power of accountability through discipleship, but instead of overcoming an addiction to alcohol, I was learning to let go of my tendency to cling to and strive for control. Those weekly meetings with Herman and my consequential growing understanding of God's Word were tangibly and practically changing my life.

Jesus's Plan for Discipleship

Herman and I continued to meet every week for the next four years. During that time, we worked our way through *Operation Timothy*, a three-book investigative Bible study published by CBMC with the goal of helping Christians lay a strong foundation for a lifetime of spiritual growth. Described by CBMC as "more than a curriculum," *Operation Timothy* is intended to help Christians grow within the context of one-on-one relationships.[7] Book 1 walks through many big-picture questions, such as what the purpose of life is, whether the Bible is credible, who Jesus is, and why He came. Book 2 focuses on understanding our new identity in Christ, fighting against temptation, connecting with the Holy Spirit, and communicating with God through prayer. Finally, book 3 goes deeper into learning how to study the Bible, discern God's will, improve our character and relationships, and disciple others. Today, the studies are offered in multiple languages, for both men and women, in print as well as digital form.

Through my meetings with Herman and *Operation Timothy*, I began to experience discipleship the way it was meant to be lived out—the way Jesus modeled for us in the Bible. Today, so many people expect their pastors or other church leaders to disciple everyone in the church through sermons and teachings, or they expect to be discipled within the context of small groups or classes. As I've already shared through stories from my own life and the story of my deceased friend Dr. Richard Edwards, the latter option usually falls short of helping individuals grow in their faith because most people don't feel safe asking or answering the truly tough life questions in a group setting. Additionally, the classroom model tends to place an emphasis on knowledge-based learning instead of practical application, which may help attendees grow intellectually but leaves them unprepared to deal with real-life challenges.

Unfortunately, the first option, in which church members rely on their pastor or other church leaders to listen to and solve all their problems, is a recipe for pastoral burnout. Not only does it require leaders to bear far more burdens than any human being is able to manage, but the reality is that many pastors and other church staff haven't truly learned how to have a personal, thriving relationship with Jesus themselves.

I have a friend who started a ministry to disciple pastors who are experiencing burnout, and he's shared with me that a big problem for more than half of the 450 pastors he serves is that they do not have an intimate relationship with Jesus. Instead of having a daily quiet time with Jesus and seeking His will for their individual lives, they focus on preparing sermons for the next Sunday and figure that will be enough. I've come to understand that future pastors often go to seminary and learn a lot about the Bible and how to preach it, but they rarely learn how to live it, much less how to teach others how to truly live it.

No wonder so many churches struggle to help people actually grow in their faith. We work hard to get people through the door on Sunday mornings, but we struggle to know how to help them after they decide to follow Jesus. Discipleship classes like the ones I attended after praying to become a Christian are fairly common, but they struggle to match the impact of one-on-one relationships. Instead of becoming active disciple-makers, believers remain passive consumers, growing in knowledge but lacking spiritual insight and conviction.

My friend Jerry Wells, a pastor here in Oklahoma City, shared with me his experience of how discipleship can be difficult to implement on a broader scale within churches—but also why he believes it is deeply important to find a way past those obstacles:

> During the time that I was a senior pastor, there were three different men in my congregation who were arrested for sexually molesting their own children. All three of these men went to prison for their crimes. The effects of the sin of these men upon their children cannot be made right by any punishment in this world. Those children were wounded and scared for the rest of their lives by the conduct and the betrayal of their fathers.
>
> As the senior pastor of the congregation in which these crimes occurred, I took these men's failures very personally. This happened under my watch as a shepherd of God's flock. I never saw any indication that any of these three men were being tempted by this kind of evil conduct. I was shocked and devastated along with these men's families and the rest of our congregation.
>
> As a senior pastor, I personally regretted the fact that I did not have the opportunity to help these men with their moral struggles before they were guilty of any misconduct with their children. After I became a senior pastor, I always had a few men I was personally discipling. We shared life together every week in a way that I came to know everything about them. Over time, I saw how these discipleship relationships and the truth that we shared helped those men grow strong spiritually to resist and overcome their personal temptations to sin and how it saved them and those they might harm from immoral misconduct. It grieved me that I could not have this

kind of relationship with every man in our church, and it especially grieved me that I did not have it with those men who had violated their children.

For years, I wished that I had a way to reproduce in the church what I was only able to do with a few men. After the failures of the three men I mentioned, I prayed even more earnestly that God would show me a way to help us create a culture in which every adult in our church would have the opportunity to be in a discipleship relationship with at least one other person. I knew that if there was a way, it would not only cause the kingdom of Jesus to grow faster through His church, but it would also prevent so much pain and suffering from happening to the families and the members of our congregation.

God has answered my prayer. Our church now has a culture in which every adult has the opportunity to be in a discipleship relationship with at least one other person. As a result, the kingdom of Jesus is growing, our church is growing, and families are being saved from the sins that are destroying our society.

What I learned through my relationship with Herman is that Jesus gave us a model for discipleship. He preached to a lot of people, but he only discipled twelve. His approach focused on the transformative power of relationships instead of only prioritizing intellectual growth. He called each of those twelve to follow Him closely, living life with Him 24/7, whether that meant eating with Him, talking with Him, listening to Him preach, or camping in the countryside and discussing the day over the campfire. Perhaps most importantly, Jesus regularly asked His disciples personal and challenging questions. He didn't live life on the surface. Instead, He probed deep into their thought lives. His teaching was compassionate, practical, and applicable, preparing his disciples to face hardship and to live out their faith daily.

After three and a half years with His disciples, Jesus was crucified and rose again, but before returning to His Father in heaven, He gave His disciples this command: "Therefore go and make disciples of all nations, baptizing them in the name of the Father and of the Son and of the Holy Spirit, and teaching them to obey everything I have commanded you. And surely I am with you always, to the very end of the age" (Matthew 28:19-20 NIV). Perhaps the most convincing proof of the effectiveness of Jesus's model of discipleship is that His disciples obeyed this command. His teaching had prepared them to become disciple-makers themselves, and they went throughout the world, spreading the good news of His life, death, and resurrection. They all faced trials and persecution but remained convinced of the truth, with most of them dying violent deaths because of their faith.

I don't think Jesus could have been any clearer. Personal, one-on-one discipleship is essential. It is God's model for life change. How else but through one-on-one discipleship, walking life for life with another believer, could you expect to learn to "obey everything" God has commanded us in Scripture? I should know—my biblical, one-on-one relationship utterly changed me, the way I think, and my life.

The Transformative Work of Scripture Memorization

At the end of four years of meeting with Herman, we'd also reached the end of the material in *Operation Timothy*. The thought at the time, from both CBMC and Herman, was that after completing the *Operation Timothy* Bible study series, someone should be ready to move on from being discipled to discipling others. Almost from day one, Herman had told me, "You really only need to be one chapter ahead of someone in *Operation Timothy* to disciple them." I felt far less certain about that. Did I really know Scripture any better than the men I might disciple? I was sure I would be asked questions I couldn't answer.

But after a couple years of meeting with Herman, I went ahead and began discipling one or two other men. The process still seemed intimidating, but the meetings seemed to go well for the most part.

So, four years into meeting with Herman, we had finished *Operation Timothy*, and I'd been discipling men for two years. From Herman's point of view, I was well on my way to life as a thriving disciple of Jesus, so he let me know we were done with our weekly meetings.

Honestly, my first thought was that at least I wouldn't need to get up for a 6:30 a.m. meeting every Wednesday. Jasco was keeping me busy as always, and it would be one less thing I needed to worry about each week.

But about six months later, Herman and I had lunch together. Partway through, he said, "Why don't you give me a couple of the verses you've been memorizing?"

"I'm sorry," I said. "But since you and I quit meeting, I haven't been reviewing my verses."

I could instantly tell my response had upset him.

"What do you mean you haven't been reviewing the verses? You've got to review your verses, or you'll lose them."

I felt like I was being chastised by my dad. I knew keeping up with my Scripture memorization was important, but I just wasn't in the habit of doing it, especially without someone to hold me accountable.

This experience is one of the reasons I now firmly believe we need to be discipled throughout our lives, not just for a few years. No man or woman can reach complete maturity in Christ after only four years.

Our need for someone to speak wisdom into our lives and to hold us accountable to the things Jesus teaches never goes away.

The rest of my lunch with Herman went fine, and not long after that, he introduced me to a man named Dan Williams. Dan was the president of a large corporation in Oklahoma City, a former marine, and a long-time member of The Navigators, another disciple-making ministry. After our first meeting, Dan asked if I would be willing to meet with him on a regular basis. I agreed without taking much time to think about it. Little did I know then that Dan and I would end up meeting on Tuesdays at 6:30 a.m. for the next twelve years.

In retrospect, I think God probably influenced my reaction and caused me to agree. He's not through with me yet, and He *definitely* wasn't through with me back then. God knew what the future looked like, and He knew I would need more training to face it.

Not only was Dan a disciple-maker's disciple-maker, but as a former marine, he was also incredibly disciplined. Where Herman had taught me humility, Dan taught me diligence in following the Lord. He had a regimented way of approaching our time together with a specific focus on spiritual disciplines, such as prayer, worship, and the study of Scripture. He wanted to hold me accountable for my spiritual disciplines, but he also wanted me to hold him accountable for his. In addition, he also gave me tools to help me succeed in those disciplines.

More than anything else, Dan was going to be sure that I memorized Scripture and that he held me accountable for reviewing those verses regularly. Soon, he had me following a pattern where I memorized one or two verses every week. The first day I worked on a verse, I would say it over and over thirty times, and then I reviewed it every day for sixty days. Eventually, I'd have a backlog of memorized verses that Dan made sure I reviewed every month so that I wouldn't lose them. Decades later, the discipline I'd learned in military school was coming back to help me, and I was incredibly grateful.

Today, the Scripture I've memorized is my greatest asset. At seventy-seven, I don't always remember people's names, but I know my verses—hundreds of them. The whole book of James, the book of Philippians, all of Romans 8, plus many others. I would not trade my memorized Scripture for anything because God is constantly bringing verses to mind when I need help or when I have the opportunity to help others. The consistent way that both Herman and Dan taught me to hear, read, study, memorize, meditate on, and apply Scripture has been a bigger blessing than I ever could have imagined when I first started meeting with them. Memorizing Scripture affects the way I think, the way I act, and the way I pray. The way I think today is nothing like the way I used to think when I was in my late thirties. My mind has been transformed by God's Word (Romans 12:2).

I share these stories in depth because I know in my core that the life change I've experienced is available for anyone. Whether you've seen a history of addiction in your family or have struggled with your mental health, I believe that learning to truly follow Jesus through the context of a one-on-one discipling relationship has the power to change the trajectory of your life. As you experience deeper connections with Jesus and with a person who really sees and knows you, as you bathe your mind in Scripture and memorize and meditate on it, as you learn to turn every problem over to Jesus with thanksgiving and trust Him for the outcome, your life will change. I guarantee it.

And if I may add one more note on this: If you are a church leader, we desperately need a discipleship revolution in our culture. If you haven't personally been discipled, I urge you to find someone a little further along in their faith walk and ask them to begin meeting with you. I believe that experiencing the power of discipleship for yourself is the best way to help that learning trickle down into the lives of the people you serve. Remember, Matthew 28:19-20—which says, "Therefore go and make disciples . . . teaching them to obey everything I have commanded you"—is directed at all Christians in your congregations and not just you as their pastor.

I grew up attending church. I'd heard many of the Bible stories before. I'd searched for meaning and purpose anywhere and everywhere. I had prayed to receive Christ in three different evangelical churches, plus at the CBMC breakfast, but those prayers didn't change my life.

My life changed the morning I started being discipled.

I owe everything to Dr. Herman Reece and Dan Williams. Both poured their lives into me through the context of the Scriptures. They taught me how to truly follow Jesus. They taught me to study, meditate on, and memorize Scripture. They asked me the toughest of tough questions about my actions and my thought life. And they helped me identify my primary sin issues, the most predominant of which was (and still is) anxiety.

As I experienced a true and intimate relationship with Jesus, learned to trust in His lasting love, and soaked my mind in Scripture, my anxiety and my fear of losing people I loved faded. I was happier—truly joyful, deep down, not just saying that I was—and more peaceful. Any time a stressful situation came up, I was able to return to the verses I had memorized, thank God for what He was teaching me through that situation, and surrender the problem to the Lord.

But as I was about to discover, the changes weren't limited to my personal life. Soon spending time in Scripture would entirely revolutionize the way I approached business as well.

Chapter 6

The Surprising Path of Stewardship

During those first few years of being discipled and studying Scripture deeply for myself, God slowly transformed the way I thought—about myself and my identity in Him, about my role as a husband and father, and even about my role as a business owner. Romans 12:1-2, in particular, stood out: "Therefore I urge you, brethren, by the mercies of God, to present your bodies a living and holy sacrifice, acceptable to God, which is your spiritual service of worship. And do not be conformed to this world, but be transformed by the renewing of your mind, so that you may prove what the will of God is, that which is good and acceptable and perfect."

I knew I needed to present *myself* to God as a living sacrifice, but I soon became convicted that that wasn't enough. As the Lord of my life through the presence of His Holy Spirit in my heart, God deserved control of *everything* I had. Over and over, God highlighted this truth for me: He created everything, and as my Creator, *He* is the rightful owner of everything I achieve and everything I possess. And that includes Jasco. He is the true owner of my business. I began to wonder: *If God owns the business, who owns the profits? Who am I to tell people that God owns my business but I can do what I want with the profits?*

After much prayer, I called our CFO, Scott Busby, into my office. This was near the end of 1997, about six years after I became a Christian and started being discipled by Herman and then Dan.

"We're going to start giving away 10 percent of our profits this year," I told him.

His jaw dropped, and understandably so. That year we had become over-inventoried in products that weren't selling quickly enough, and we had almost as much debt as we did assets.

"Steve, we can't do that," Scott said. "We owe too much to the banks. We need every penny we can get our hands on to pay down our debt."

He was right that we needed the money, but I'd already been praying about this for months. I knew God was calling us to begin tithing on our corporate profits. Throughout Scripture, we read that, as Christians, we are to pour ourselves out for others, not only with our time but also with our treasure. As Jesus told His disciples, "If anyone wishes to come after Me, he must deny himself, and take up his cross and follow Me. For whoever wishes to save his life will lose it; but whoever loses his life for My sake will find it" (Matthew 16:24-25). I knew without a doubt that giving 10 percent of our profits was something God had put on my heart and that I needed to be obedient.

However, I was still terrified.

As midnight neared on December 31, 1997, I found myself holding what was, for me, an astronomically large check. My plan was to deposit it in a donor-advised fund at the National Christian Foundation, which would allow us to donate all the money at once and then allocate the funds to different charities over time.

Whenever I retell the story, I like to dramatize it a bit and say I had a death grip on the check that New Year's Eve. But that's not far from the truth.

Why would anyone ever give away this much money? I thought.

But my conviction held true, so I let the check go.

Meanwhile, God was working behind the scenes. A few months earlier, I'd loaned my friend Randy Marx a fairly large sum to help him finance the production of some of the products Jasco was purchasing from his company. Randy insisted on giving me some shares in his company's penny stock that was traded over the counter as a thank-you. I tried to refuse because he was paying us the market rate for interest, but he insisted.

"I've always wanted you to own shares in our company," he said. "Please take it."

I accepted, but I didn't think much about it after that.

On January 12, 1998, twelve days after I let go of that large check, Scott Busby came into my office.

"Steve, you remember that stock that Randy gave you back in October?" he asked. "It went up to $1.24 per share this morning."

"Oh really?" I replied. "What does that mean?"

"It means it's worth about seven and half times the amount we just gave away to charity."

"What?" I was stunned.

"Yeah," he said. "What do you want me to do with it?"

"Sell it!"

Scott sold our stock, and a few days later, the price went back down to a few pennies per share. I called Randy and asked if he had any idea what made the stock rise and fall so suddenly.

"Steve, I have no idea," he said. "It just went up—surprised me too—and then went back down. There's no rhyme or reason behind either of those things."

But I knew the reason.

Paul writes in 2 Corinthians, "Now He who supplies seed to the sower and bread for food will supply and multiply your seed for sowing and increase the harvest of your righteousness; you will be enriched in everything *for all liberality*, which through us is producing thanksgiving to God. For the ministry of this service is not only fully supplying the needs of the saints, but is also overflowing through many thanksgivings to God. Because of the proof given by this ministry, they will glorify God for your obedience to your confession of the gospel of Christ and for the liberality of your contribution to them and to all" (2 Corinthians 9:10-13, emphasis added).

In only twelve days, God had given Jasco back more than seven times what He had put on my heart to give. Not so that we could get more for ourselves, but so that He would be glorified and we would have more to give away. It's a lesson I've continued to see evidence of for years since then: The more you give, the more God will give you to give.

We have no need to waste time worrying about the future. God has everything under control, and when we surrender to Him, He does more than we could have imagined on our own.

Trusting God with Everything—Even Bankruptcy

Corporate giving wasn't the only challenge God presented us with in 1997. Earlier that year, I got a call from Steve Birke, the vice president of consumer electronics at Target.

"We need you to come to Minneapolis," Steve said. "Something's come up."

A couple of days later, I hopped on a plane to Minneapolis and walked into a conference room to find all of Target's buyers for consumer electronics as well as Steve Birke. I could already tell something was up.

Usually I met with one or two buyers directly, not with all of them and certainly not with Steve, the head of the division.

Steve got right to the point. "Jasco has been a great supplier to Target for twenty-five years, but the brands you have just aren't cutting it anymore. We need you to get the rights to a top-tier name brand, otherwise we won't be able to do business with you anymore. We're going to give you sixty days to come up with a solution."

Swallowing hard, all I could say in that moment was, "Okay."

The whole flight home, my mind raced. As I've already mentioned, we were over-inventoried in the wrong products that year. We were highly leveraged. I didn't have the foggiest idea where to go to get a top-tier name brand. And since Target represented 60 percent of our business at the time, I just didn't see how we could survive without them.

When I got home that night, I went to my knees.

"Father," I prayed, "You know that I'm very concerned and tempted to be anxious but thank You for the challenge. Show me how to take Jasco through bankruptcy with integrity because we're about to lose 60 percent of our business. Or if You don't want me to do that, then we need a top-tier name brand, and I have no idea where to go to get one." I sighed. "I surrender it all to you."

Then I went to bed and got an unbelievably good night's sleep. A few years prior, sleeping peacefully in a situation as dire as this one would have been unthinkable. I would have been up all night worrying and scrambling to come up with a solution. But now, after six years of discipleship, I was able to rest and surrender Jasco's future to the Lord.

The next morning, I got up and went into the office. The phone rang as soon as I arrived. It was Steve Birke again.

"I want to introduce you to someone at Thomson Consumer Electronics," he said. "I think you might want to go talk to them."

I wasn't entirely sure why Steve wanted me to meet with Thomson. I knew Thomson owned the RCA brand, so I thought maybe he wanted Jasco to distribute the RCA brand to Target for Thomson. There was a possibility that might fulfill Target's demand for Jasco to get a top-tier name brand, but I wasn't sure how it would all play out. So, a couple of days later, I got on another airplane, along with our vice president of marketing, Kent Shiplet, and we went to meet with the folks at Thomson, prepared to pitch our services as distribution partners. Imagine our surprise when we got into the room and the team from Thomson handed *us* thick folders with a well-laid-out pitch.

"I don't know if you know or not, Steve," said Jack Nick, the head of Thomson's accessory division, "but we have the rights to the General Electric brand as well as the RCA brand. Though we market GE televisions, we're not marketing accessory products under the GE brand, and we're wondering if you'd be interested in licensing the GE brand for accessory products from us."

I *hadn't* known they had the rights to the GE brand for our categories. I think I must have been sitting there with a puzzled look on my face because I felt Kent elbow my side.

"Take the GE brand," he hissed.

So I did.

Only eleven days after I met with Steve Birke in Minneapolis, Jasco attained the worldwide rights to the GE brand name for all of our categories of electronic products.

Witnessing God at Work in Hindsight

At the time, I knew that God was the one who brought GE to us. He was the one who preserved Jasco and gave us the means to continue growing and expanding. But, in the years since then, it's been amazing to hear even more about all the ways He was working behind the scenes.

Jasco's former chief marketing officer Bill Otte worked for one of our competitors when the GE deal occurred. At the time, Bill never would have dreamed of working for Jasco, but God had different plans. Bill tells the story best, so here's what happened in his words:

> In the early 1990s, there were two mega giants in the consumer electronics accessories business: Gemini Industries, which handled the mass market side of things, and Recoton Corp, which focused on more specialized products. And then there was this little company called Jasco, which was a pain in the butt because they held the bulk of Target's business. I joined Gemini in 1994. Gemini did a lot of work with Target, but we never could get the core of the business. That was always Jasco.
>
> In 1996, Gemini had just acquired the licensing rights to Magnavox, which was a top name brand like Sony and RCA at the time. I remember sitting in a meeting with Steve Birke (Target's head of consumer electronics), one of Target's buyers, and Gemini's VP of sales as we pitched our Magnavox products to them.
>
> "You've got the Emerson and Southern New England Bell brands," our VP of sales said. We knew Jasco had recently acquired those brands—in fact, it was part of what pushed us to go out and get Magnavox. "We're here to offer you Magnavox and Southwestern Bell."
>
> Our brands were huge compared to the ones Jasco had access to. Target would be crazy to say no.
>
> But their buyer asked us, "What will happen if I say no?"

Our VP of sales looked him straight in the eye and said, "If you tell me no, I'm on the next plane to Bentonville, Arkansas. We'll sell to Walmart instead."

I wasn't privy to all the conversations Steve Birke had with Steve Trice and Jasco at the time. All I knew was that a couple of weeks later, Jasco somehow had the GE brand, and Target had cut a deal with them.

GE had even better brand awareness than Magnavox. I remember thinking, *What?! Jasco has GE?* I was so frustrated.

Gemini's VP of sales stayed true to his word. We went to Walmart and started selling Magnavox products to them. Eventually we were able to sell headphones to Target, and we did close to $40 million a year with them, but we could never get rid of Steve Trice. We approached Target probably four times in the next two or three years, offering them deals that would cut Jasco out of the business, but we couldn't unseat them.

Finally, I went to my boss, the CEO at the time, and said, "This is really simple. Jasco's a single account. You go and sign a three-year deal with Target at cost. Steve Trice can't afford to meet competition at cost. Drive him out of business."

"Bill," my boss said. "Sometimes if you corner a badger, it fights back."

"Not if you kill it," I replied. "Dead badgers don't fight back."

My boss decided against my advice. Instead, he called Target and told them we wouldn't be coming back to them anymore because every time we presented them with new ideas, they took them and gave them to Jasco.

The irony of my journey is not lost on me. I'm the evil one in this story, saying to my boss, "Kill Jasco." But God's response to my efforts was really simple: "No." Who would have guessed that, fifteen years later, I'd be working for Jasco as their chief marketing officer?

I worked for Gemini for several more years before we were acquired by Philips. For a couple of years, I frequently traveled to Europe on Philips's behalf. There, I'd get up on stages and talk about how well we were doing as a company. We were like the goose who laid the golden egg at the time—we were just killing it. But eventually Philips consolidated their offices, which meant I'd have to move if I still wanted a job. I decided to leave. After that, I worked a different (horrifyingly bad) job for a couple of years before quitting that too.

As I was searching for new opportunities on LinkedIn one day, a CMO job popped up for my archenemy, Jasco. Although I'd competed with them for years, I could tell the role would be a good fit, so I decided to give it a shot. Three hours after I sent in my résumé, Cameron Trice called me.

"Why don't you come on in for an interview?" he said.

At some point during the interview, Cameron asked, "Why did it take you so long to apply for the job?"

"I've been looking for six months," I replied. "It just now showed up on my LinkedIn."

"Well, we've had it posted for a year," he said.

Within weeks, I was Jasco's new CMO.

All I could think was, *That's got to be God*. Jasco couldn't fill this position for a year until I finally found their LinkedIn ad and applied.

In a final bit of irony, Philips had slid from a $750 million business to a mere $5 million business over a ten-year period. Shortly before I joined Jasco, Gibson Guitars acquired Philips and agreed to let Jasco sublicense the Philips brand and become their sole distributor in

North America. That meant that when I came on as Jasco's CMO, I was once again responsible for the brand I'd helped grow years earlier.

If you don't think God played a part in all of that, then you're not paying attention. It's just too bizarre, and I blame God for all of it. He protected Jasco through everything. I learned the hard way that if God says, "You're not putting them out of business because you're going to work there in fifteen years," then you're not putting them out of business. Jasco is *His* company, and we're here to steward it.

Walking with God Through Seasons of Growth

Getting the GE brand allowed us to begin selling to all the major retailers—Walmart, Amazon, Lowe's, The Home Depot, Walgreens, Best Buy, Costco, and Sam's Club, among others. The GE brand had huge name recognition, but it had never included accessory products such as connecting cables, jacks, and plugs for TVs, stereos, computers, and other categories we served. Thomson wasn't interested in adding those categories at the time, but we were already manufacturing those products under our own brand names. All we had to do was add a GE line of products to those categories using the same manufacturers but different packaging. By licensing GE from Thomson, Jasco began expanding rapidly, growing from a $20 million business to a $50 million business over the next seven years.

Then in 2004, Mary Newell-Miller, the president of GE licensing, contacted me through Jack Nick at Thomson and said she'd like to meet with me. I took Jasco's marketing director with me, and we flew to Princeton, New Jersey, for the meeting.

"Tell me a little about Jasco," Mary said as we sat down.

I did, and she listened, nodding and asking questions occasionally. Then she asked me to walk down the hall to her office with her. Inside, she had a whiteboard, and on it was written "Jasco—HEP?"

What is HEP? I wondered.

"We know about the success of Jasco and what you've done with GE's brand through Thomson," Mary said. "We'd like you to consider buying our home electrical products business."

It was an enormous offer. GE's home electrical products (HEP) business, which included things like light switches and dimmers, light fixtures, timers, surge protectors, extension cords, etc., was worth $100 million in sales at the time. But it also came with huge obstacles. To buy their inventory, Jasco would need to raise $60 million, and the most we had ever borrowed was $17 million. We would need a new warehouse approximately twice the size of our current one. We would need to hire an additional one hundred people. And we would need to complete all those things within ninety days so that we could take possession of all the HEP products from five GE warehouses.

Before starting down the path, I wanted to be sure it was the right decision. Acquiring the GE licensing had convinced me that God was in control, and if He wasn't behind this HEP deal, I didn't want to do it.

By that point in my walk with Jesus, I'd learned to follow a biblical model for decision-making that I adapted from one developed by George Müller, a nineteenth-century Christian evangelist:[1]

1. Seek a frame of mind through prayer where you truly have no will of your own but only want what the Lord wants.

2. Search for any Scripture passages that relate to the subject of your decision and study those closely, praying through those verses and seeking wisdom from God.

3. Consider the positives and negatives of each possible decision.

4. Seek wise counsel.

5. Turn everything over to the Lord, asking what He would have you do.

After praying, studying Scripture, and seeking wise counsel, I've learned that the answer usually comes. As a final step, I remember the words of Isaiah 30:21: "Your ears will hear a word behind you, 'This is the way, walk in it,' whenever you turn to the right or to the left." I apply this verse by praying, "Father, I've made my decision. Here it is. I hope that it's from You, but if it's not, help my ears to hear a word behind me: *This is the way. Walk in it.* If this isn't from You, please put a check in my spirit."

For the HEP deal, I decided to take things a step further and put a figurative "fleece" before the Lord as Gideon did in Judges 6. I would ask NeAnn and a handful of other wise counselors what they thought I should do. If even one of them said no, then that was the end—it wasn't meant to be.

I honestly figured NeAnn would say no. After all, I was fifty-seven, and we had been talking about early retirement since I was forty-five. But to my surprise, the first words out of her mouth were, "We've got to do that!"

"Are you sure?" I said. "Do you know how much work it will be for us to buy a company twice as large as we are?"

"But think about the ministry opportunities and how much more we'll be able to do," she replied.

Each of the other people I went to for advice all said I should go ahead with the deal. I never felt like God gave me any checks—or hesitations—in my spirit either, so we began to move forward. But first, we still had to find out if we could borrow $60 million to buy the GE inventory.

When I went to see Jasco's bank lending officer, Ty Downs, and explained to him what we needed, his first response was, "That's more money than we're going to be able to lend you. But," he continued, "if you'll give me a place to work at Jasco for a couple of hours every morning for the next few days, I'll come out there and get on the phone and call some banks around the country. We'll see if we can put together a consortium of banks to work together and loan you the money."

And that's what he graciously did.

Meanwhile, we still needed to find a larger warehouse to store all the new merchandise. We looked at every available warehouse in Oklahoma City, and none of them would have worked except one. It was on sixty acres with plenty of room for growth and only one mile from our headquarters at the time. It was already set up with all the specialized shelving we needed to store pallets of products, and it was owned by a friend of mine, Mike Dillard. We needed several special concessions to work out a deal, and Mike was willing to meet them all. The warehouse was the perfect place for us to move. We sold the location we'd built on 122nd Street and moved everything to the new warehouse on Memorial Road—the facility we still have today.

With the acquisition of GE's HEP division, our business tripled overnight and has continued to grow. All the details fell into place perfectly, and I believe wholeheartedly it's because God was over every single one of them.

Even now I tell these stories and can only shake my head in awe over the way God works. I was never smart enough to start a company as great as the one Jasco has become. God put the idea for Jasco on my heart and provided all of the necessary financing and the customer base.

I didn't search for the GE brand. I didn't ask about buying the HEP business from GE. I didn't make phone calls to gather money for the loan we needed. God did it all—I just showed up. That's one of the many surprising things about walking with God: You do the best you can to steward what He's given you and then you get the pleasure of watching Him do more than you can imagine.

God was in control of it all. He always had been, but at last I could see His hand clearly.

Chapter 7

You Can't Outgive God

Several years before the HEP deal, around 2000, Dan Williams had been discipling me for about five years, and I was on fire for the power of discipleship. I had begun discipling two or three guys myself by this point and loved the encouragement I found through mentoring them in their walks with Christ. I found myself wanting to disciple even more men on a regular basis, but I didn't know how that would be possible considering how much of my time still went to running Jasco.

So, later that year, I talked to Larry Lide, who was Jasco's general manager at the time, and I asked him to become CEO in my place so that I could spend my time discipling more people. He agreed, but he only had that role for about six months before he came to me on a Friday afternoon.

"Steve, I've got a problem," Larry said. "I'm going to need to have triple bypass heart surgery on Monday."

Thankfully his surgery was a success, but not long after that, Larry ended up leaving Jasco altogether in order to start his own real estate business. Initially, I was frustrated because I had no choice but to resume being the CEO. But then God impressed a new truth on my heart: *Steve, if and when I want you to disciple more people, I'll make that possible. For now, Jasco is your full-time ministry.*

The ministry that grew out of that realization was two-fold. First, we had already begun tithing on corporate profits, which allowed us to do a lot of good for many Christian nonprofits. Second, Jasco employed around one hundred people at that time, and I realized we had the opportunity to share the gospel with and provide discipleship opportunities for all of them.

I began to develop a new mission statement for Jasco. We would be "a company dedicated to facilitating the growth of God's Kingdom through servanthood in the marketplace as He may lead." That meant embracing generosity and a servant's heart both within Jasco as we cared for employees and outside of the company as we cared for our buyers, our customers, and the ministries we had the opportunity to support.

If you're in any kind of business, whether you're a boss or an employee, I imagine you might be asking yourself, "How much difference can one company make?" My answer to that question would be that any company, large or small, can make an immeasurable difference not only in their community but in the world as a whole—as long as that company is completely surrendered to the leadership and ownership of God.

My hope is that the following stories will prove that point.

Put People Over Profits

Before I became a Christian, if anyone would have asked me what my greatest asset as a businessperson was, I would have given a quick-and-ready reply: "People." But in the back of my mind, I knew that what I was doing was just leveraging people to make money for myself and my family. I think this can be a temptation for many people in our society. Materialism dominates our culture, and any amount of success in business can easily lead to a drive for more—and more, and more.

For me, after I came to know Jesus personally, I experienced a complete mindset shift. By this time, I'd already learned to prioritize my family over my work, giving them my real time instead of my foldable time, which had always been my dad's struggle. Recognizing that God owned everything, including Jasco and all of its profits, was another huge milestone in my journey. Anything "more" that I earned became one more way I could honor God and give back to Him for Him to do with as He wished. Giving generously became a joy—and interestingly, giving also became a way of dealing with my anxiety. The more I gave, the more I learned to trust God's provision, which dramatically lowered my tendency to worry over the future.

As my hold on Jasco's profits and on money in general eased, rather than focusing on what my employees could do for me, I began to deeply care about them as individuals—about their relationships with Jesus, their spouses, their children, and their money. As a business, Jasco has the privilege of getting people's time during their best hours of the day. I began to wonder: *Why not use those hours to do everything we can to teach them about a relationship with Jesus Christ?* I wanted every team member at Jasco to be able to grow into all God created them to be.

The chance to begin using Jasco as a ministry and to care for our people well came very soon after my conversion. Not long after I started meeting with Dr. Herman Reece, he came into my office one day and said, "I want to start a weekly prayer group for CBMC, and I noticed you have a conference room right down the hall. Could we use that room for the group?"

I agreed without hesitation and soon joined the group myself. Sometime later, Herman, who was CBMC's metro director for Oklahoma City at the time, asked if he could use a spare office at Jasco for his CBMC work. Eventually, CBMC of Oklahoma City began officially officing out of Jasco and still does today. But that was only the start. Beginning in 1994, the executive team and I started praying at both the beginning and end of company-wide meetings. Often in those meetings, I or another Christian leader would share the gospel or talk about how our faith impacted various decisions we were making. We even hired a company chaplain to minister to people one-on-one and to lead optional Bible studies for those who were interested.

Eventually, we began including significant prayer time during weekly executive meetings, during which we prayed extensively for our team members. Now in 2025, we have 350 team members, though that number has been as high as 500 in the past. With a group of people that large, there are always several who are struggling. Over time, our executive team has discovered that these prayer meetings not only encourage our employees, but also have the power to change our hearts as leaders and help us be better prepared to love and serve our team members. While the members of our leadership team aren't perfect, they always do their best to care well for the people God has put in our path.

> "I love how the executive team is intentional every week to pray for employees who are going through tough times. If you've ever been on that list, you'll sometimes get a text from an executive—'Just checking in on you,' or 'Just want to let you know we're praying for you,' or 'Hey, I heard the good news,' or whatever it may be. I think any person at their core appreciates that. I've been on that prayer list, whether it was when I lost my dad or when I lost my mom. Just to get those texts, to have the flexibility when they say, 'Go, take care of that. We've got this.' When somebody's in a very tough situation, they want you to have that time and flexibility to go take care of what's important."
>
> —JEFF CATO, VICE PRESIDENT OF MARKETING AND E-COMMERCE

One of our corporate values is that we embrace diversity and foster an inclusive environment of respect and dignity for everyone. That means that we're very careful to make sure our employees know all these spiritually related opportunities are optional and not a requirement for anyone's job. It's a delicate balance, but we do our best to make sure everyone understands these things are voluntary. We don't want to push anyone to do or believe anything—we merely want to make the materials available and let them know about the difference Jesus has made in the lives of many of Jasco's leaders.

As we grew in our desire to view Jasco as a ministry and to serve our team members well, we developed our What Matters Most initiatives to care for our employees in a holistic way. These initiatives are our attempt to go beyond training our team with job-related skills and invest in the whole person of every member of our team by giving them opportunities to grow spiritually, emotionally, physically, relationally, and financially. For example, in addition to chaplain services and Bible studies, if any employee wants to take his or her spouse to the Weekend to Remember marriage retreat put on by FamilyLife, a ministry of Cru, we pay their registration fees and the cost of their hotel, plus provide a stipend for a date night during the weekend. We also provide retreat fees and paid time off for a Christian women's retreat and men's retreat, as well as one for single moms.

To help our employees grow physically, we have a walking trail, a multipurpose sports court, and a state-of-the-art fitness center with weekly workout classes on Jasco's campus. Our breakrooms include a fresh market stocked with sandwiches, salads, and other healthy choices for employees to purchase, and we host various sports and fitness challenges and competitions throughout the year to encourage team members to get moving. We are a smoke- and tobacco-free campus, and we host on-site biometric screenings, mammograms, and PSA screenings, as well as a vaccine clinic that employees can participate in at no cost.

> "How do we run our business every day? I think there are two things: generosity and servanthood.... Steve Trice has set the stage for us to give back to the community. Providing support to charitable organizations is a wonderful feeling as we strive to help others who are less fortunate. In addition to helping others, our mantra of leadership through servanthood is a key driver as to how we serve both internal and external customers. We have an obligation to exceed expectations through excellent customer service. It is just what we do!"
>
> —Mark Schaffner, VP of Product Development

To promote community health, we offer regular volunteer opportunities, host quarterly blood drives on-site, and have a committee of people who are willing to help their fellow team members in times of need. In the interest of helping employees grow professionally and develop financial wellness, we offer monthly lunch-and-learns on a variety of topics, provide financial and retirement planning services, and host Dave Ramsey's Financial Peace University on-campus annually. Additionally, we provide financial assistance to team members who are pursuing higher education.

We also try to involve our employees in our corporate giving as much as we can. We offer both "Dollars for Doers" and "Dollars for Donors" programs through which we donate to charities where our employees volunteer as well as match any donations they make. We've heard from many employees over the years that involving them in the giving process in these ways has created a greater sense of purpose in their work. While we always want to make high-quality products, if our mission as a company was only about selling light fixtures and surge protectors and HDMI cables, that would be good, but it's so much greater to be able to share the gospel and help people who need food, shelter, and water, and to give God the glory for all of it.

A Deep Sense of Accomplishment
by Preston Nuckols, Associate Product Manager

The fact I didn't finish school has always been a hole in my soul. Not having my degree felt like a dark secret that I never really talked about. Anytime I'd go to dinner with someone and the topic of college came up, I usually tried to change the subject. But then Jasco announced at their annual company-wide meeting that they were starting a new program and if anyone wanted to go back to college, they'd help us finance it. So I made the decision to try again—for probably the sixth time by this point—and went back to college at fifty years old.

At fifty-two, I received my associate's degree. At fifty-four, I received my bachelor's. At fifty-six, I received my master's. And now, at sixty-three, I just completed my PhD. And Jasco paid for everything—registration fees, books, and classes. In my calculation, it cost them about $130,000 to put me through school.

Having my degrees has changed my life. Knowing I was able to accomplish each of those programs has changed the way I look at myself. Now when I lie in bed at night, I have a deep sense of accomplishment. When I was a kid, I used to pray for knowledge, wisdom, and understanding. To be able to go back to school and get my degrees has transformed me from feeling like a peasant to feeling

> like royalty. If someone asked me today, "Would you rather have a million dollars in the bank or a PhD?" I'd say I would rather have that PhD.
>
> I've been with Jasco for twenty-two years now. As a company, Jasco is always encouraging us to take opportunities to develop ourselves and to become better people. It's one thing to educate myself, but it's another for my company to teach me to become something greater. Jasco and its leadership are teaching me to nourish and develop my soul as a person—that's one of the reasons I think people like working for the company and continue working for them for so many years.

Corporate generosity has its challenges. For one, it's so countercultural that it can initially sound quite foreign to employees. We always strive to be generous and fair in our compensation; however, I'm sure some Jasco employees have occasionally wished we'd use some of the money we give away to raise their salaries instead. But overall, I've been incredibly impressed and blessed by our employees' responses to our generosity as a company. I think most people really enjoy working for a business they know is making a difference in a positive way.

> "Every day I walk in the door, I make money for the company, and I help someone I don't know. What could possibly be better than that? Even on a bad day, I'm still helping somebody, so it's a great day."
>
> —BILL OTTE, CHIEF MARKETING OFFICER, RETIRED

Rather than being a hindrance, I believe our focus on generosity as a company has helped us recruit and retain great talent. While I once said our people were our greatest asset somewhat automatically, without giving it much thought, now I fullheartedly believe it. Our people are everything. We couldn't do what we do without great people. And that means that we always strive to prioritize people over profits.

"As the generosity team overseeing giving at Jasco, we may not be dealing directly with Jasco's customers or business partners, but we consider Jasco's ministry partners to be our customers, and we aim to provide exceptional customer service to them. We don't want giving to be transactional. We don't want to just say, 'Well, here's your gift. Talk to you in a year.' We spend a lot of our time actually meeting with our ministry partners, especially if they're in Oklahoma City, but virtually, if not. For those that are local, we go on site visits. We organize volunteer days for our team to go pitch in and help them out, and that allows our team members to also get to know and become familiar with some of the organizations that Jasco supports and partners with. Generosity can come in all forms, so we really love it when we are not just giving them a financial contribution but are able to support them in other ways as well."

—CELENA MCCORD, DIRECTOR OF GENEROSITY

When We Surrender, God Moves

From the time we began tithing on our corporate profits in 1997, we gradually increased the percentage of money we gave as God led. We continued to donate through the National Christian Foundation and had dubbed our donor-advised fund the Jasco Giving Hope Foundation. By 2008, we were giving away about 25 percent of our profits, but then the Great Recession, as it was called nationally, arrived, which meant consumers were generally buying less from retail stores. Our sons, Jason and Cameron, were both involved in the business by that point, and we got together to talk and pray about what to do, considering we might experience a near-term business loss.

The answer we received from the Lord was the one we least expected: *Double your giving.*

On a practical level, it didn't make any sense. But the three of us became very convinced that God did, in fact, want us to double our giving, so that year we gave away 50 percent of our profits.

During the next four years, our market share increased faster than it ever had before. I've calculated that it took only about thirteen months to make up the difference from doubling our giving in 2008.

Ever since then, our aim has been to give away 50 percent of our profits. And we've been able to do that every year except one. We always make sure our giving is in line with the business metrics for the year and that we still have enough to reinvest in the business, but 50 percent is always our goal. That number has worked well for us—not only is it the maximum tax-deductible donation we're able to make, but also the remaining 50 percent has proven to be just enough to pay taxes and still grow the company. Effectively, then, God receives all of Jasco's available profits.

> "When people ask, 'What do you do?' I say, 'I work for Jasco. I do corporate generosity. We give away 50 percent of our profits.' And they're like, 'Fifteen?' 'No, fifty.' Really, it's unheard of. Nobody believes it. We use the phrase 'irrational generosity' a lot, and when I was interviewing with Jason, that phrase really resonated with me. I've always kind of thought, If I'm not worried about myself, if I'm just focused on taking care of others, then nobody has to hoard resources, and they have the same philosophy. We just all trust that there are sufficient resources and support for everyone out there. So, it's not a scarcity mentality. I love that."
>
> —AMANDA HOWELL, GENEROSITY COORDINATOR

Over and over, God has proven to us that we can't outgive Him. The more we give, the more He gives us to give away.

One challenge along the way has been discerning how much to share about our giving with employees, customers, buyers, and the general public. For many years, our executive team knew about our giving, but few employees knew, and our customers certainly weren't aware. I wasn't necessarily trying to keep it a secret, but telling others wasn't a priority. At some point, my family and I also began to ask ourselves if it was best to keep our giving anonymous as Jesus says in Matthew 6:3-4: "But when you give to the poor, do not let your left hand know what your right hand is doing, so that your giving will be in secret; and your Father who sees what is done in secret will reward you."

But over time, we began to see the encouragement our employees and customers might also receive through knowing they were helping to support so many nonprofits and consequently large numbers of people in need. We were also instructed by Matthew 5:14-16 when Jesus says, "You are the light of the world. A city set on a hill cannot be hidden; nor does anyone light a lamp and put it under a basket, but on the lampstand, and it gives light to all who are in the house. Let your light shine before men in such a way that they may see your good works, and glorify your Father who is in heaven." Ultimately, we decided that it would be worth sharing about our giving as long as we made it clear that we were trying to glorify God and not ourselves.

Over and over in Scripture, God speaks about how we are to love in a generous way, pouring ourselves out for others. As Jesus says in the Gospel of John, "This is My commandment, that you love one another, just as I have loved you. Greater love has no one than this, that one lay down his life for his friends" (John 15:12-13). We are to lay down our lives for others, to give out of both our time and our treasure. For me, one of the biggest ways God has called me to this is through our corporate giving at Jasco. That's not me waving my flag and saying "look at me"—that's me saying I'm just doing what I've been told to do. We have been able to play a small part in the work of dozens of wonderful ministries over nearly thirty years, and watching their good work in the world has consistently reminded me of the power of generosity. I'm incredibly grateful and humbled by what God has chosen to do through our small company.

"I am forever grateful for that very first 'yes' Jasco gave Pearl House. It has launched others to also say yes, and it has provided opportunities for so many in Ghana to say yes to Jesus. Pearl House now serves over five hundred students, employs over seventy Ghanaians, counsels hundreds of girls with trauma, and provides hope to so many in Ghana. Lives are being forever changed, voices of empowerment are being given, education is being received, healing is being created, hope is being established, and an environment and atmosphere that radiates the love of Jesus is being felt! Jasco has been a faithful foundation for Pearl House and has continued to walk alongside us, creating new opportunities for us to serve others well."

—Courtney Bullard, Founder and Chief Visionary Officer of Pearl House

"Through Jasco's incredible generosity, we were able to bring Oklahoma's only Best Buy Teen Tech Center to our Northeast Boys & Girls Club location. The Teen Tech Center helps close the opportunity gap, providing hundreds of teens access to innovative technology, which allows them to find their passion and puts them on the path to a great future. Jasco didn't simply write a check and step away. They have been active in the

Teen Tech Center throughout the entire process, even sending employees out to volunteer regularly and mentor our teens. Without their partnership, this amazing resource simply wouldn't exist, and we are so grateful for their continued support."

—Teena Belcik, President and CEO of Boys & Girls Clubs of Oklahoma County

"City Center's journey with the Jasco Giving Hope Foundation began with a simple conversation with Jill Trice, a volunteer at the Center. She and her husband, Cameron, made a generous donation to support our efforts, and then later, she introduced us to her father-in-law, Steve Trice, and Giving Hope. When Steve and I met, I shared my vision for Oklahoma City and the hope to serve at-risk youth and families with dignity through City Center. As we discussed the challenges and opportunities ahead, I could feel the alignment of our hearts and missions. But Steve left me speechless at the end of our meeting when he offered to give us enough money to buy the building we were currently renting from a local church. That moment marked a pivotal turning point for City Center. This gift freed up resources that allowed us to have a permanent home and to move on to serve thousands of under-resourced families and underserved youth through community-based initiatives, having a truly rare impact in Oklahoma City and beyond."

—Jed Chappell, Founder and CEO of City Center

One of the best examples of this that I can think of is our partnership with Water4, a ministry that works to "build and scale durable market-based water businesses that create more: safe water access, economic opportunity, virtue, and purpose across Africa."[1] As of the end of 2024, Water4 has helped provide:

- 836,500 people with access to Water4's NUMA-branded piped water systems and 2,644,904 people with access to safe water sources, including handpumps

- 14,969 active NUMA water points and 21,304 all-time water projects

- 1,284 people with ongoing jobs in NUMA businesses

Water4's NUMA approach focuses on getting treated water to rural homes that is then purchased for a fee, which enables a regional business to thrive. Half of the 836,500 people who benefit from NUMA-piped water are women and girls who used to spend three hours a day fetching water from unsafe sources. That means those women and girls combined now have over 1 million hours a day back, hours that can now be used for their education, livelihoods, health, and spiritual lives.

But what I love most about Water4's ministry is their discipleship-driven approach. In addition to starting for-profit water companies that help provide clean, piped water throughout sub-Saharan Africa and create job opportunities for thousands of people, employees of Water4's water businesses participate in "discovery Bible studies," an oral, inductive Bible study process. They learn to retell Bible stories in their own words and to consider what the stories teach about God and about humanity, what the story is prompting them to do, and who they might share the story with in the next week. For many of those employees, the Holy Spirit has often placed one of the many thousands of customers the business interacts with on their heart, which begins a new cycle of reading, interpreting, obeying, and sharing inside communities where they work. This peer-to-peer discipleship method has led to massive multiplication. Water4 currently tracks more than 30,000 active weekly discipleship groups through their ministry, with more than 158,000 confirmed weekly attendees. More than 1 million people have heard the gospel through their work, and close to six thousand have been baptized in the past two years.

"Over the eleven or twelve years Jasco has been supporting us, there have been moments when we felt a lot of pressure from outside sources to focus only on water infrastructure and the water utility side of what we do and take out the faith-based part of our organization. But both Steve and Jason have reminded us that this is God's company, God's mission, and God's resources, and that we need to stick to this dual calling of both business and mission and trust that everything we need will be provided. They have enabled us to stand firm in our belief that God desires to make disciples through our work of water. In an industry and culture where people are increasingly uncomfortable with faith, Jasco's practice of being a world-class and excellent company while being bold in their faith set a clear and constant example to us that the Lord would provide all we need to achieve His vision."

—MATT HANGEN, CEO OF WATER4

As I think about the thousands of people who are being served every day by the ministries like Water4 that we have the privilege of supporting, I can't help but think back to where it all started when Herman Reece first entered my office. Did he have any idea that day that thousands, if not millions, of people would be touched by the gospel because he was willing to give of his time and disciple this one guy?

I doubt it.

But that's what God does when we surrender to Him.

As Isaiah 60:22 says, "The least of you will become a thousand, the smallest a mighty nation. I am the LORD; in its time I will do this swiftly" (NIV).

The question I asked at the beginning of this chapter—How much difference can one company make?—comes to mind again now. Like I said before, if that company is surrendered to God, then the difference is immeasurable. But I would also ask you to consider: What difference can one *individual* make when he or she has surrendered completely to God's leadership and guidance?

Again, I would suggest that the difference that an individual can make is immeasurable.

The Gift of Education
by Robin Khoury,
Founder and Principal of Light Christian Academy

I hurried into the lobby of Jasco to meet my friend Dr. Herman Reece. Dr. Reece was helping us get Little Light Ministries and, specifically, Light Christian Academy, our school for children of the incarcerated, up and running. By this point, we had been working toward opening the school for three years while we ministered to women incarcerated at the Mabel Bassett Correctional Center in McLoud, Oklahoma.

This was my very first fundraising appointment, and I was nervous and excited. I hurried to the appointment, being certain not to be late. (On "Herman time," if you're not ten minutes early, you're late.) Herman was waiting for me when I arrived. A few minutes later, Steve Trice came out to meet us and invited us into his office to visit about our dream of a free, private Christian school for children who had been affected by incarceration and poverty.

Mr. Trice asked me about our vision. I shared how God had spoken to me years earlier that someday I would start a school for disadvantaged children. This calling was confirmed in different ways and later clarified to become a school for children whose parents had a history of incarceration. Mr. Trice looked at the little budget I had typed out.

"How much have you raised so far?" he asked.

I felt myself blushing. "Well, you are the first person we have asked."

"How is that going to work?" he replied. "It's already June, and you are starting in August."

I thought for a moment. "Well, we don't have to have everything we want to start," I said. "We have our meeting place and our students. I have been a homeschool mom, so, if necessary, I will get pencils and paper and go up to the church and start teaching them on the first day of school."

That day was a Friday. By the next Wednesday, we had received a check from Jasco fully funding our first year, as well as a generous matching grant to help us begin our community fundraising efforts.

We started in the fall of 2012 with six students and ended the year with only three. But we kept going. Each year we added a few students and lost a few. As we went, we learned how to better teach children who have been exposed to trauma. We learned how to run a Christian school and how to show the love of Christ to our students and their families. After five years, we outgrew the little church we had started in.

After an extensive search for an appropriate property, we found a nine-and-a-half-acre campus in the exact neighborhood where we wanted to be. In a surprise move, Jasco purchased the property for us, which allowed us to use the other funds we had raised to refurbish the buildings. When Mr. Trice called to let us know about the gift, I sputtered out, "Thank you—I don't even know what to say."

"We have to take care of these kids," he said.

Light Christian Academy has now been in existence for twelve and a half years. We have served hundreds of children during that time, providing them with the gifts of literacy and education, warm coats, hot meals, and the love of Jesus. Today, Light Christian Academy is fully accredited and serving forty-four students. Our first high school senior graduated in May 2025. We value our sustaining relationships with the Trice family and Jasco. We thank God for their faith in God's provision and their generosity to the least of these among us.

Light Christian Academy exists "to raise followers of Jesus that are academically and spiritually prepared for life."[2] The academy provides students with free tuition, meals, uniforms, transportation, and school supplies, made possible through donations and grants. Learn more at lightchristian.academy.

From Money to Mission

I'd love to share one final story with you—one of my favorites. It was about twenty years ago now, when a Jasco employee named Anthony asked me to come by his office one day because he wanted to share something with me.

My first thought was, *Uh oh. What happened?*

But when I went into his office, he said, "I just want to tell you about something that happened here. You shared the gospel one day in a meeting, and I prayed to receive Christ."

If that had been the end of the story, I would have been thrilled. But Anthony went on, explaining that he had then taken his wife to a marriage conference that Jasco sponsored, and she prayed to receive Christ too.

And he still wasn't done.

"That's not what I brought you in here to tell you though," Anthony said. "Last night, I went to tell our eight-year-old daughter good night and to tuck her in. I walked into her room, and she'd fallen asleep with her children's Bible on her chest. She'd been reading her Bible—not because her mom and I wanted her to but because she wanted to. That's the difference Jasco has made in my family's life."

To me, it doesn't get any better than that. Jasco has become a ministry, and stories like this are what ministry is all about. It's about loving people well and doing everything we can to introduce them to the joy and fullness we have experienced in God and to help them grow in a relationship with Him.

I'm amazed by all the changes that Jasco has gone through since its founding. As I've already described, in my early days at Trice Wholesale Electronics, the environment was completely different, with a strong focus on smoking, drinking, and making money. As far as I know, before I became a Christian, the only time God's name was mentioned at Trice or Jasco was in vain. Now we consider God the owner of everything we do and produce. Prayer is a regular part of the workday, and while we still want to make a profit, our primary motivation is continuing to make a difference in people's lives through the many wonderful organizations we support.

It's a miraculous change indeed.

But in those early years after I became a Christian, there was still one more miracle I was praying for: that my sons would come to know the same life-changing love I'd experienced in Jesus.

Chapter 8
Entrusting Your Family to God

Our sons would tell you today that they were raised in church, but looking back, I wish I'd done things differently. The church NeAnn and I took them to during their growing-up years didn't provide a strong foundation for their faith. Jason and Cameron heard a lot of good stories on Sunday mornings, but those stories weren't going to lead them to Christ any more than they had led me to Christ.

But then, all of a sudden, when I became a Christian in 1991, all I wanted to talk about was Jesus. From my perspective, Jesus had become very prominent in my mind, and I wanted Jason and Cameron to know Him too. But from their perspectives as an eighteen-year-old and almost-sixteen-year-old, respectively, I'm sure it seemed that I had totally lost it and become a Jesus freak.

One verse in Proverbs that has come to mean a great deal to me says: "Train up a child in the way he should go, even when he is old he will not depart from it" (Proverbs 22:6). I've taken that to mean that there could be many years when young men or women may not act in line with how their parents had hoped, but, if they were raised with faith in God, they'll eventually return to the truth. I took comfort in that hope as I spent the next ten to twelve years praying for my sons' salvation.

I could try to summarize the changes I eventually saw take place in their lives, but I think it will be far better and more meaningful if I let them share their stories themselves.

> ### Leaning Away and Then Back In
> ### by Cameron Trice
>
> When I was growing up, we were "Sunday Christians," if you will. We went to church most weeks, but we didn't talk much about faith at home or crack open the Bible as a family or do any kind of active discipleship. When Dad went through his spiritual transformation and got into one-on-one discipleship, his demeanor as a dad somewhat changed. But what sticks out most in my memory was how his faith impacted his relationship with my mom. He started talking about how he wanted to love her like Christ loved the church and be there for her through her ups and downs and lay himself down for her.
>
> At the time, my main thought was, *Whoa, whoa. You don't want to be a doormat, Dad.*
>
> However, I did start to notice a difference in his attitude—he was no longer depending on my mom for his happiness. And he didn't seem to be depending on Jasco either. As he has often told us since then, much of his anxiety had faded away.
>
> I was already close to sixteen when Dad had his conversion experience, so it was only a couple of years later that I headed off to college. I attended Southern Methodist University in Dallas, but there was very little that was overtly Methodist about the school. It was very secular—no Bible classes required.

I decided to double major in philosophy and business. I'd picked up the study of philosophy partly because it seemed like a good counterpoint to a business degree, especially if I decided to go to law school after college. In my classes, we read everyone from Plato to Aristotle to Nietzsche—all the great thinkers. Reading those classic philosophical arguments was fascinating to me, especially after experiencing a more conservative upbringing. I enjoyed exploring their various points of view, but one thing that stuck with me throughout my studies was that none of these philosophers seemed to have any consensus on truth. Their view of the world was extremely relative. They sounded good saying it, but I was skeptical that their type of worldview would take me very far.

Growing up, between Jason and me, I'd always been the one who interrogated my dad about what was going on with Jasco, from the time I was twelve on into high school. I worked in the warehouse in high school and put thousands of Christmas stickers on packages being shipped to Target or Service Merchandise or Montgomery Ward. Later on, I worked in accounts payable, accounts receivable, and data entry. I was interested in coming back to Jasco after college, but my dad had made it clear to both my brother and me that while he'd love for us to work there someday if that's what we wanted, he'd like us to get at least two years of experience somewhere else first after college.

So, after I graduated from SMU, I went to work as a legal assistant for Baron and Budd, a law firm in Dallas that, at the time, focused on representing asbestos victims. The environment there was a little like the *Mad Men* days at Trice Wholesale Electronics. They had a keg on the floor, open-bar parties, and all sorts of drama and soap-opera stuff going on between the partners and interns.

Around the time I was wrapping up my second year at Baron and Budd, my dad got the call from Steve Birke and learned that Jasco might lose Target's business. I was keeping tabs on the situation from down in Dallas, and I remember thinking that I didn't want to jump on a sinking ship. I wasn't sure if the family business was still going to be afloat in a couple of years, so I began making plans to get my JD/MBA at the University of Texas.

But then, the next thing I knew, Jasco licensed the GE brand, and the company's future seemed to be on much better footing. A few weeks later, I got a call that an assistant product manager position was available at Jasco if I wanted to apply.

I thought, *Why not?* Even if I decided to go ahead and pursue my JD/MBA in a couple of years, I knew working at Jasco would be a good experience. I figured I might as well try my hand at the family business.

Little did I know I would never leave. I started out in product development, and I've mostly stayed in that arena ever since. I've always loved the creative aspect of developing products, and even today as co-CEO, I spend a good portion of my time doing that. It's what I'm drawn to, and it's where I feel I add the most value. However, after my first couple of years at Jasco, I also started traveling to Minneapolis regularly with my boss, Kent Shiplet, to meet with Target buyers. Eventually, I had the opportunity to take over sales responsibilities from Kent. I thought long and hard before accepting that opportunity because I knew how much pressure that job would bring, but I've ended up being incredibly grateful for the experience I gained in that role.

Although I probably viewed myself as somewhat agnostic during my years at SMU and Baron and Budd, I'd never completely departed from the Christian foundation I'd been raised with. If anything, I felt a bit conflicted. However, returning to Jasco in 1998 brought many new opportunities to lean back into my childhood faith.

By this time, Dad had already introduced a value-based culture with a Christian foundation into the company. While I didn't report to him directly, he was certainly a mentor to me during my first few years at Jasco. I'd often hear him retell the story of how his life had been changed through a relationship with Jesus and one-on-one discipleship, and how God had saved Jasco by bringing the GE brand to the table. He'd always been a good marketer and storyteller, but I could also tell what a true difference his faith had made in his life. I'd inherited Dad's tendency to be anxious, and hearing how God had helped him deal with the really tough possibility of losing Jasco was especially meaningful. While he'd always been a good dad in my view, it was clear he had become a very different guy over the past decade than he'd been when we were growing up.

My dad wasn't my only Christian influence at Jasco, though. We had weekly prayer meetings as part of a normal company rhythm, and I began to notice and admire how many other Christian leaders were at Jasco as well.

I'd seen how one-on-one discipleship changed my dad's life, so relatively early on in my career at Jasco, I started meeting with Jim Kimball, our COO at the time. We would meet at Panera each week to go through *Operation Timothy*. We memorized Scripture and read books together, but it was pretty casual. We'd also spend a lot of time talking shop. As I look back now, that was kind of the 101 discipleship class for me.

Meanwhile, I realized that while I'd studied some brilliant philosophers at SMU, none of them seemed to agree on much of anything. But now I began to find some brilliant Christian philosophers as well, like C. S. Lewis, who had arrived at the strong belief that there *is* moral right and moral wrong and that Christ is the source of truth. This seemed like a stronger spiritual foundation I could build my life on.

Shortly after returning to Oklahoma City, I moved into an apartment complex on 122nd Street. One day while I was shoveling snow off my car, I noticed a young woman about my age clearing off her car nearby. Our gazes caught, and we both laughed. I saw her a couple more times near the apartment mailboxes. Finally, one day when I was coming home from work, I saw her sitting on the apartment stairs chatting on the phone. She had a dog with her, so I decided to use that as my opening.

I pretended that I liked the dog (I'd never been much of a dog person) and asked to pet it. She got off the phone, and I found out she was actually dog-sitting for her parents.

We fell into easy conversation, and eventually I managed to work in my real question: "Are you married?"

To my delight, she was single. That was all I needed to know to start pursuing her. Jill and I built a friendship first. We had a ton in common and found out we'd lived in the same neighborhood twice when we were growing up. We'd also both gone to college in Texas and were working to reestablish friendships in Oklahoma City. About six months after we met, we began officially dating, and though we weren't in a hurry, I was pretty sure Jill was the one. We dated steadily for the next several months, got engaged in December 2000, and were married on September 8, 2001.

Jill always had more of a natural faith than I did. She was certainly a positive influence on me, and throughout our relationship, the faith I'd had as a kid began to resolidify.

Jim Kimball discipled me for about three years before he retired and moved to Florida. At that point, I asked Dan Williams, who discipled my dad, if he would begin discipling me, and he agreed. Jim and I would cobble together our one memory verse for the week, but with Dan, I have about thirty verses that I have to recite in sequence. So, for the past two years, I've been taking the discipleship masterclass. But I was ready for that—it was what I signed up for, and it has been a great experience. I'm looking to take on one or two "Timothys" of my own in the near future because it's all about shepherding a new generation and modeling out discipleship. My dad modeled that for me, and I'm now living that out and benefiting greatly from it.

In my faith journey, I never had a moment when I hit rock bottom and went to my knees in surrender or rechecked the box to become a Christian. Instead, it felt more like I had leaned away from faith for a few years and then leaned back in. Between meeting Jill, being surrounded by godly leaders like my dad and other Jasco executives, and being discipled by Jim and Dan, I saw my faith begin to grow, and it has only continued to grow ever since.

One Millimeter at a Time
by Jason Trice

I've always joked that I helped to bring my dad to Jesus because I tested his faith. At eighteen, I was fiercely independent and rebellious, wanting to separate from my parents and do my own thing. We'd been Sunday church people when I was growing up, but the churches we went to were not ones I loved attending. They were the wooden-pew kind of churches with sterile Sunday school rooms. They just weren't the places I wanted to hang out as a kid. My primary memory from my childhood experience with church is hiding in bed as long as I could on Sunday mornings, hoping that my parents wouldn't come in and make me go. When my dad became a Christian as an adult, it seemed very odd to me. It certainly wasn't something I wanted to embrace for myself at the time.

On the business side of things, I started working at Jasco when I probably wasn't quite legally old enough, working in the distribution center and cutting products out of blister packages with a box cutter so they could be repackaged. They paid me fifty cents an hour, so I was both good child labor and cheap labor. Later, as a teenager, I worked for minimum wage unloading trucks. I remember being hoisted up to the top of the warehouse by a forklift one time to grab a box. I'm fairly certain that experience is why I don't like heights today. While I appreciated the chance to earn a little extra cash, I really didn't have any desire to be part of the family business long-term at that point.

In high school, I got really into debate. I was competitive, and debate was something I was good at. I liked verbal sparring, and I enjoyed researching, strategizing, and putting together arguments to win. It became something I could sink my teeth into. From very early on after I started debating, my teenage vision for my life was to become a debate coach.

After graduating high school in May 1991, I was offered a debate scholarship to Northwestern State University of Louisiana. I started out as a math major, switched to journalism, and eventually ended up in political science. Our debate team did very well, winning the overall Team National Championship for the season in 1994, but after three years, most of my friends were graduating and I was offered a debate scholarship to Michigan State. I decided to transfer. It turned out to be a great move for me because in 1995, my debate partner and I won the Heart of America Tournament and the Cross Examination Debate Association National Championship, which no team had ever done before, and again won the overall Team Season Championship in 1996.

Being part of that team was also where I met my future wife, Emily. Since we're both debaters, we've always had very healthy arguments and discussions—sometimes heated but always structured. Emily is a few years younger than me, so it took us a little while to hit it off. But by the end of her freshman year and my senior year, we'd developed a strong friendship. We worked long hours together in the library preparing arguments for debates. When her mom passed away unexpectedly several months into our dating relationship, walking through that grief together cemented our commitment to each other.

After my eligibility for debate ended, I decided to pursue my master's in communication, and I landed a job as the assistant debate coach for Michigan State in 1997. Then, in the fall of 2000, I reached my goal of being named the university's director of debate.

For a couple of years, I was on top of the world. Emily and I got married on June 3, 2000, and I loved coaching. But after a while, I realized that being the director wasn't the same as being up on stage and executing arguments. Our travel schedule as a team meant I spent lots of weekends away from Emily, and as I moved into my upper twenties, I also found it harder to connect with the freshmen coming in. I kept getting older while they stayed the same age, and I wasn't getting the same joy or camaraderie from coaching the team anymore. Additionally, the only path upward career-wise was to try to become the dean of the honors college, which wasn't something that interested me at all. I wasn't even thirty years old, but it felt like I'd capped out in my career in academia.

By 2002, I was ready to consider a change. Cameron had joined Jasco a few years earlier, and he and my dad had been trying to recruit me to come back to the company. Emily and I were thinking about starting a family, and the idea of being closer to my family in Oklahoma City and Emily's family in Emporia, Kansas, was appealing. It felt like the right time to turn a new page.

I started out as a product manager at Jasco over the computer accessories category. Ironically, this meant I reported directly to my little brother, Cameron. Though that was a bit of a challenge for me initially, I felt like we were able to build a good working relationship.

Soon, I really began to enjoy the new challenge of my role at Jasco. I spent my first few years developing products for Target, Best Buy, and Staples before becoming director of product development for the PC category. Then in 2006, I made a change and took a position on the business development side of Jasco. When the executive vice president of sales left six months later, my dad and Cameron encouraged me to consider taking that role. I certainly didn't feel ready for it, but I accepted the position with my dad and brother's support and learned some important lessons that have helped me through the rest of my career.

If I hadn't come back to Jasco, my life today would look very different. I probably wouldn't be as close to my brother and my parents because I'd likely still live far away and only visit a couple of times a year. On the personal side, Jasco also brought a lot of structure and accountability to my life. My job in debate had included some eighty-hour work weeks, but it gave me a ton of flexibility in the summers. Being at Jasco forced me to grow up and move on from the college lifestyle.

Most importantly, being part of the business influenced my faith. During college, I would say I fell away from even the basic level of faith I had as a kid, and I really struggled with it for a while, as I think a lot of people do. But when I came back to Jasco, being around my dad and my brother and other people of faith helped restore and grow my relationship with God. At Jasco, God was everywhere, and as I began to open my eyes and look around, I saw everything that He had done.

There was never a point in time when the Lord brought me to my knees, and I prayed to accept Him. I don't have some defining "this is the day I came to Christ" story like my dad has. My faith has been more of an evolution instead of a revolution. But the more time I spent in Scripture, the more He worked on my heart. I began to admire the deep faith I observed in my parents. As the saying goes, "Show me your friends, and I'll show you your future."[1] This certainly proved true in my life. Being associated with Christ-minded people at Jasco had a huge influence on me over time.

I've been in a discipling relationship with my spiritual mentor, Scott Klososky, for twelve years now. Scott was originally discipled by my dad, and his firm, Future Point of View, has served as a technology consultant for Jasco on and off over the years. He's helped coach me toward practices that have had a positive influence on my life, such as starting my day connected to the Spirit through morning meditation, spending time in Scripture, or having a conversation with God. All of these practices help me gain perspective and center myself so I'm ready to come to the office and spread His love. I'm an imperfect human who fails every day. I'm very consistent about spending time in Scripture, but then I get in the heat of meetings and I probably don't live that out the way I should. Jesus was perfect, and I am not. But I'm a huge believer in accountability partners, whether it's someone who helps hold me accountable for working out and taking care of this body that God has given me or a spiritual mentor to hold me accountable for my spiritual practices. We're all going to go through periods of adversity. I think it's good to have a relationship in which you have some level of confidentiality—someone who can do life with you and help you through grief or challenging decisions, someone to bounce ideas and joys and hurts off of. It's a blessing that makes this life more manageable.

I look at our faith journeys as a continuum where we're all walking with the Lord and sometimes we walk closer than other times. Over the past twenty years, which have included me getting married, having kids, and coming to work at Jasco, I've learned that life is about more than just me, and I've moved closer to the Lord. Just like I got to be six-foot-four one millimeter at a time, I'm still somewhere along my spiritual journey with Christ. I have a long way to go, but He has taken me pretty far from where I was as a rebellious teenager, and He's continuing to show me and teach me new things every day.

From Lukewarm Christianity to Flourishing Faith

God has blessed our family incredibly, but of all our blessings, I'm perhaps most grateful for how He has worked in our sons' lives. I'm well aware that things could have gone in a very different direction. I've witnessed first-hand in the lives of many family members and friends how painful it can be when a child strays far from the path their parents hoped they would follow. I know how easy it is in those instances to ask yourself, *What should I have done differently?* I wondered that myself many times in the years when I wasn't yet sure what path Jason and Cameron would take, and I often wished I'd been able to do more when they were young to guide them toward Jesus.

But standing where I am now, on the other side of those years, two important points stand out. First, nothing is more important to our children's faith than our prayers. We can't control the outcome—we leave that up to God—but praying faithfully for our children to learn to follow Jesus is vital.

Second, we can model our own faith by the way we live. Cameron echoed the importance of this as he reflected on how he seeks to lead his own kids now:

> If my dad had started trying to push more things with faith when we were younger, I'm not sure it would have made any difference. The most important thing he did once we were old enough to really be looking up to him as a role model was to model out his values and his faith in Christ. Now, in the same way, I can go to my kids and tell them whatever I want. I can say, "You need to do Scripture memory," or "You need to read the Bible every day." But chances are, they're going to see that as an obligation, something they're being pushed

to do. The best thing I can do for them is be an example. They see how I deal with problems, how I love my wife. Modeling that out for them is going to be a whole lot more important than anything I tell them. If I'm talking the talk but not walking the walk, chances are they're not going to walk the walk either.

I saw this truth play out in Jason's and Cameron's discipleship journeys as well. As they were beginning to grow in their faith, I offered several times to take each of them through *Operation Timothy*, but their answers were always the same: "No thanks. Sorry, Dad." Imagine my surprise, then, when each of them came to me—not very far apart—and asked if I would suggest one of the guys I was discipling to disciple them. It makes sense looking back. They didn't want Dad to disciple them. They wanted to learn from a fellow businessman. And my guess is that my asking them about it didn't influence them nearly as much as the benefits they'd seen play out in my life because of my own discipling relationships. Now, they've both ended up being discipled for years by guys I discipled, as well as by one of the men who discipled me, in Cameron's case.

Today, they are beautiful, godly men who are not only brothers but also best friends and business partners. What a God thing to see the two little boys who used to beat up on each other in the back seat arrive at the place they are now. For more than ten years, Jason's and Cameron's families lived three blocks from each other, and within the past couple of years, they both bought new houses that are now two doors down from each other. Their kids have grown up so close to each other that they are more like siblings than cousins. I have lunch with Jason every Monday, and NeAnn and her mother have lunch with Jason on Tuesdays. On Fridays, Cameron comes over to our house to have lunch with both NeAnn and me. NeAnn and I usually get to see our grandkids every week too, and our whole family will go out to the lake for a few days multiple times a year. The tradition started many years ago when NeAnn and I would take our two little boys to camp in a tent at the lake. Today, we've upgraded to condos, but we still treasure that time together.

NeAnn and I have also been privileged to see hints at redemption and new direction for our siblings' children, grandkids, and great-grandkids. All of our siblings and many of their children have had struggles of their own, including many divorces. About twenty years ago, NeAnn and I prayed and felt led to do what we could to step into the gap for members of the youngest generation. We offered to pay for private Christian education for any of those kids whose parents decided to take us up on it. Two of NeAnn's nephews have gone all the way through K-12 Christian private schools and have now graduated from Christian universities. And this past spring, I received a text from my sister's great-granddaughter, who likewise attended a K-12 Christian school and just graduated from Liberty University, a Christian college in Virginia. The text contained a picture of her boyfriend, who also graduated from Liberty, down on his knee asking her to marry him. They have since gotten married. I'm touched that we've been able to play a small part in the lives of those great-nieces and nephews, and I pray in hope that these young people will be able to experience God's lovingkindness for all of their future generations (Exodus 34:7).

Not many people get to grow in their faith as much as I have after getting started at age forty-three. After all the brokenness and pain of my childhood, to see my family flourishing and the company I steward for our Lord making a difference in the lives of so many people is more than I could have imagined. And it's all because God, who was always in control, sent one man into my life to disciple me.

Little did I know how much more God still had planned. Only He could use a consumer electronics company to influence generations to come.

Part 3

Legacy

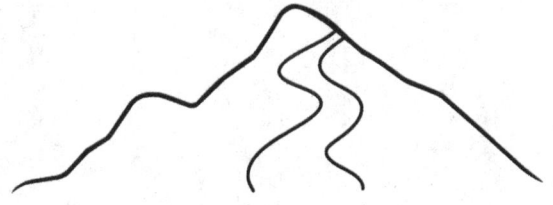

Chapter 9

Nurturing Next-Gen Leaders

On average, family-owned businesses last about twenty-four years.[1] Although the US is home to more than thirty million family businesses, only about 30 percent are successfully passed on to a second generation, and only 12 percent reach the third generation.[2]

I'm sure you could talk to a dozen different family business owners and get a dozen answers as to how they've successfully transitioned their businesses from one generation to the next. But as I reflect on my own family's journey, a few key principles stand out. In particular, (1) we've always tried to prioritize our family relationships over the ins and outs of the business; (2) we've worked together to create clear vision, mission, and values statements that have kept us all on the same page as we transitioned to the next generation; and (3) we've surrendered ownership of our company to God, which means we entrust Jasco's future entirely to Him. You'll find stories of how these principles have played out in our family throughout this chapter, but I would like to suggest up front that the last point is, in my opinion, by far the most important to keep in mind and seek to implement. Unless we surrender our families, our careers, and our businesses to God, all our efforts to preserve a legacy for the next generation will likely come to nothing. But when we give ownership to God and trust Him with the outcome, we experience true freedom and thriving.

Teaching Hard Work, Not Entitlement

Though I always hoped that our sons might come back and join the family business, the goal was never to get them into Jasco. What was most important to me was that they came to know Jesus and then followed their passions and did what He wanted them to do. Once it became clear that they both *wanted* to come back to Jasco, I was thankful and thrilled. But I also wanted them to gain experience and work their way up in the company before entrusting them with too much leadership.

From the time Jason and Cameron were young, NeAnn and I did our best to teach them the value of hard work and money. We gave them small weekly allowances for doing chores, and they both worked summers at Jasco from an early age. As Jason approached his sixteenth birthday, NeAnn and I initially disagreed on how to handle getting him a car. Though I didn't plan to buy him a Corvette like my dad had done for me, it seemed reasonable to buy him *a* car. But NeAnn disagreed. She hadn't gotten her first car until she was twenty-one when she'd earned enough money to buy one used. Until then, she caught rides with friends or took the bus. Although she'd hated it at the time, in hindsight, she appreciated the lessons about thriftiness she had learned along the way.

Ultimately, we compromised. We bought Jason and later Cameron cars for their sixteenth birthdays, but we required them to give us a down payment and then make monthly payments to us until the car was paid off. Without them knowing it, we deposited their checks into separate bank accounts. When they graduated from college, we gave them access to those accounts to give them a little help as they got started on their own. By that time, they'd each built up a nice little nest egg from the car payments they'd paid us over the years.

> "I feel incredibly blessed that my parents did a lot of things, things I probably didn't even realize at the time, that didn't make it feel like we had a silver spoon. We went to a great private school, but we didn't feel wealthy compared to some of the other kids because mommy and daddy didn't just give us new red BMWs for our sixteenth birthdays. I got my mom's used car, and I paid for it. There are a lot of things that my parents did that Emily and I are doing with our kids. It's about passing on that value of hard work, and it's not about just earning money. It's about adding value to this world and others, whether that's for yourself or your family or those around you. I want to enable our kids to chase their dreams, whether that's Jasco or music or wakeboarding, but I don't want to enable them to do nothing and just travel the world as 'trust fund kids.' We're always trying to strike that balance and teach them the value of hard work."
>
> —Jason Trice

As you've already heard from Cameron in the previous chapter, I also told my sons that I wanted them to work somewhere else for at least two years following college before possibly returning to Jasco. That was a lesson I'd learned from my dad. He didn't require me to do that—I started working for Trice Wholesale Electronics immediately after college—but he always said it was good for kids to go work for somebody else for at least two years before returning to the family business. I'd heard the same advice when I was part of the Young Presidents Organization, a leadership community for chief executives, and I agreed it sounded like a good idea. By the time each of them returned to Jasco, Cameron had worked for two years at Baron and Budd, a law firm in Dallas, and Jason had worked as a debate coach at Michigan State for five years.

"My dad, in my view, did a really good job with me. Of the two of us, I was the one interested from early on in coming back to Jasco, but it was never an expectation that I would work there. And even if I did, the idea that I would own or inherit or be entitled to anything was never a concept or a conversation. I was expected to go get an education and some work experience, and then I might have the opportunity to work at Jasco, but I would have to start at the bottom like anybody else and work my way up on merit, not on my last name."

—Cameron Trice

Over the next sixteen years for Cameron and twelve years for Jason, they worked their way up in the business until they were both on my executive staff. By 2014, Jason was running the sales team as the executive vice president of sales, and Cameron was the executive vice president of product development and marketing. At the time, I was only sixty-seven and hadn't thought much about retirement, recognizing that there is no retirement discussed in Scripture but only changes in God's calling on our lives. But I also remembered how my dad had struggled to have a future vision for his company at age seventy, so I knew I didn't want to be CEO much past that age.

I believed either of my sons would be a capable leader. But which of them would be right for the role of CEO? They had such different strengths. Jason was the older brother and was great with the financial and operational aspects of the business. On the other hand, Cameron had been with Jasco a little longer, and he was creative and innovative in product development. In any personality test they take, Cameron tends to be cast as a pioneer, a visionary known for creativity and forward-thinking, while Jason is often pegged as a guardian, someone who safeguards values. Both qualities are needed in a CEO. My health was still good, and I wasn't in a hurry to retire, so I didn't feel like this decision needed to be made overnight. However, I began to make plans to have both Jason and Cameron take some spiritual gifts tests in hopes that the results would help me see who had stronger administrative skills. Maybe that son could become CEO and the other could take on the COO role.

But then Jason and Cameron came to me with a proposal: What if they became co-CEOs?

My initial thought was that I'd have to pray about it. I'd never heard of co-CEOs, so the idea felt strange. But my sons had come to the discussion armed with stacks of articles and stories of co-CEOs of other businesses who had been quite successful. It turned out they'd been thinking about the idea and discussing it for a year or more. By that point, they were prayerfully united in their belief this would be a good solution. There were pros and cons, but being co-CEOs would allow both of them to focus on what they were good at. Additionally, they wanted me to stay on as the chairman of the board so I could monitor their governance and settle any disagreements that came up between the two of them.

As I usually do, I followed the biblical model for decision-making I'd learned years ago. I began studying the idea of co-leadership in the Bible and found the examples of Paul and Barnabas, and Paul and Silas. I sought wise counsel. NeAnn thought it was a good idea—she knew how hard I had to work to handle the CEO role on my own and thought it would work nicely to have Jason and Cameron split the role. I talked to a friend and well-known business leader to get his perspective. He was skeptical initially but ultimately said that if it didn't work out, I was still young enough that I could pick up the leadership role again myself and find another solution. By the end of a few months of prayer and consideration, I felt God prompting me to move forward with Jason and

Cameron's plan. In 2014, they became co-CEOs, and I transitioned to become chairman of the board.

"Usually, the second generation is where the business fails. I've known many an entrepreneur who's started their business and worked 24/7 to make sure it was successful. And then the kids come in, and they don't have a clue. They're kind of spoiled, and they don't really care about the business. What I appreciate about Jasco is that both Jason and Cameron are fundamentally as in tune with the business as any second generation I've ever seen in my life. Cameron is a product guy. He's a tinkerer. He's an innovative mastermind. He is involved in every aspect of the business.

He is totally immersed, and it's part of what he does every day. And Jason is the ultimate debater—he'll question you a thousand which ways to Sunday. He's a tough guy, but he's a genuine person. He wants that interaction, he wants you to be able to think things through, and he'll challenge you. He's more direct, and I like that. . . . I've got to tell you, the second generation is usually out there having fun—this second generation is top notch."

—MARK SCHAFFNER, VP OF PRODUCT DEVELOPMENT

Prioritizing Family Bonds over Business

In our family, we've always worked hard to put our relationships with each other ahead of the business, and Jason and Cameron have continued that pattern in their roles as co-CEOs. Jason manages operations, finance, and the Giving Hope team, while Cameron focuses on product development, sales, and marketing. They'll tell you that dividing up their areas of responsibility has been a key to success. Instead of worrying about redundancies or disagreements, they tend to defer to each other on their areas of expertise.

I asked them for their thoughts on how they keep their relationship as brothers as the most important thing, and Cameron shared this:

Ninety-five percent of things we agree on anyway. But if we do need to have something out, we hash it out behind closed doors. Then on weekends or Thanksgiving or Christmas when we're with family, we're with family. That family part of the relationship is by far the most important thing. We don't have to talk about work at all. But at the same time, we enjoy talking about Jasco and strategy, and we talk quite a bit of shop. The work side of it can almost enhance the personal side of it because we have this thing in common—we're partners in business. So you navigate any disagreements and say, "What benefits the relationship first?" and make sure the business side of it doesn't negatively impact the personal side of it.

Jason added these thoughts:

The business has been a blessing for our family as a whole. Cameron went to college in Dallas, and I went to Louisiana and Michigan. I think there's a low probability that both of us would have come back to Oklahoma absent the magnet of Jasco. To me, they go hand in hand, and for the past twenty-plus years, I've just looked at my brother as my brother, best friend, and business partner. We're close. Most weeks we have lunch, and we talk about personal stuff, but we also talk about business. That's one of the things we've got in common, and for the most part, it's a blessing. He and I are very different. He's more creative. I'm more business by the numbers, and that creates different perspectives. I think there's strength in both, so we just work to reconcile those things. We occasionally have disagreements, but we really haven't found a whole lot over the years that we can't resolve over a couple of glasses of wine. There's occasionally some things that we just have to agree to disagree and respect that he runs his area of the business and I run mine.

If Jason and Cameron do find themselves stuck on a disagreement, we have a larger advisory board made up of experienced business people and entrepreneurs who can offer advice and help them find a solution. In my continuing role as chairman of the board, I also frequently talk through ideas, questions, and concerns with them and can act as a mediator or tiebreaker if necessary—though the number of times I've had to do that in the past ten years has been very low.

I'm so glad we moved forward with making Jason and Cameron co-CEOs because it has worked out phenomenally well. They're very different leaders, but they're both bright, articulate, and good with people. Their strengths are extremely complementary to each other. And they're doing it all in the name of the Lord. Our sons are not only brothers but also best friends and business partners who are stewarding this business God has given us into the next generation. Knowing this is one of the greatest gifts I could have imagined.

"Jason and Cameron are like brothers to me—they're that close to me personally. In my first year working at Jasco, a decision was made that affected me greatly in a negative way. I remember telling my wife, 'I love working here so much, and yet if I can't resolve this, then I don't know if I will be able to stay at Jasco." Her response was, 'You need to talk it out.' I remember I asked for a meeting with both Steve and Jason, and they let me speak my mind for about thirty minutes. After I had explained my point of view, they gave me their perspective. I didn't necessarily agree with their viewpoint, and I'm not sure if they agreed with mine. About three or four weeks later, Jason came back to me and said, 'OK, here's what we're going to do,' and it was a good solution. That was just my first year of working here, but there was so much anguish in me because I couldn't imagine leaving. It just hurt, and I was so relieved to solve it. Now, Jason and I look back at that, and we're both so glad we worked it out. This is the longest I've ever worked somewhere, and it's without question the best place I've ever been."

—Mitch Loukota, Executive Vice President of Sales

"I've never seen Jason and Cameron not honor their word. Let me put it that way. One of the things that really stuck out to me that shows—day in, day out—how they do things is that right at the beginning of the COVID epidemic [in 2020] when there were a lot of unknowns and a lot of pressure points in so many areas, they went ahead and raised the pay for the distribution center workers.... In the midst of a lot of uncertainties and not knowing what the future would hold, they said, 'We need to up the pay and take better care of our DC employees.' That says a lot about them because I think that was a time when companies were doing the opposite, if anything. I think it goes back to the fact that they were really trying to do what they felt was right."

—Jeff Cato, VP of Marketing and E-Commerce

Leading Out of Your Strengths

One of my favorite things about Jason and Cameron's co-CEO relationship has been watching them grow and deepen in their individual leadership strengths. Cameron continues to act as a pioneer, developing new products and marketing strategies while also seeking to care for and mentor our employees. Here's how he describes one of his favorite initiatives:

A few years ago, I started doing Coffees with Cameron, so anyone in the company can schedule a coffee with me. It went against every bone in my body when I first started because I'm a big introvert, and I was really reluctant to open up my schedule to everyone. But I decided it would be a good way to keep me informed and engaged.

At the beginning, I aspired to make the coffee with an espresso machine, but that got to be a lot of work, so now we go to Starbucks and I get them whatever they want coffee-wise. Many people have told me that at previous companies, they had no access to the CEO. Some people really want to engage, and some don't. But for the ones who want to engage, whether they have an idea for a change in the business or just want to get to know me a little better, those coffees have been very beneficial. Often we end up talking about family and personal life, and lots of times I find out that person needs to be on the prayer list for Jasco executives, which we go through every Monday morning. Even though I was reluctant at the beginning, Coffees with Cameron has become the most informal and approachable tool I have for building relationships with and mentoring people at Jasco.

Jason, meanwhile, seeks to steward our resources well, making sure that Jasco stays true to its mission and using his ability with numbers to watch over our giving initiatives through the Jasco Giving Hope Foundation. Here's how Jason explains his involvement with the foundation:

> Each executive at Jasco has a strategic initiative they're responsible for championing, and mine is the heart of Jasco. That means I seek to keep us on track with why we do what we do. It's the Lord's business, and we steward it for Him so that, God willing, we have the ability to support those in need in our community and spread the good news of Jesus. My dad used to steward our giving through Giving Hope all

on his own, but over time it's grown beyond what any one person can do. We hired a part-time employee to help him with that in 2018, and then in 2021, we hired two generosity ambassadors to oversee Jasco's giving full time. I meet with them weekly, leveraging my strength with numbers to help develop a framework for our giving.

We've also worked to formalize our giving processes more in recent years. I think it's good to have disciplined approaches with Giving Hope and some goals for developing a reserve in case the business goes through a tough year or two. Although we hope to provide steady support to our ministry partners, we don't want a ministry to become too dependent on us. We want them to have the sort of diversity and solid foundations that Jasco is always seeking as a company. Additionally, although we're not always able to help every time a natural disaster or international crisis occurs, by giving generously throughout the year, we hope to enable our ministry partners to be ready to act when the need arises.

In addition to my work with Giving Hope, I've had the privilege to be on the board for Water4, one of the nonprofits we support, for the past nine years. I was able to go on a vision trip to Rwanda with Water4 in 2017, and I learned a ton about their approach. Their mission strikes a bunch of sweet spots for me. One of my passions is dual-purpose missions, and Water4 does that by providing clean water as well as spiritual water. Plus, they operate like a business—they're working to gain scale, and they aim to give hand-ups instead of handouts. Water4 drills wells with materials that can be locally sourced. They also charge a small amount for the water so that the people they serve value it more and they can create a revenue stream to help maintain the well long-term. It's a game-changer in terms of community development.

I would say Water4 has impacted me more than I've impacted them, but I feel like I'm able to add some value from a business and marketing perspective as part of their board, even if I don't understand how to drill a well. I'm grateful for the ability to play a small part in ministries like Water4 through Giving Hope, especially because I'm very aware that it's not the Trices giving to these ministries. The money and resources all come from God, and we give all glory to Him for the ability to give generously. My family and I are just stewarding those resources.

Creating a Vision for the Next Generation

As our family has worked to transfer leadership to the next generation, I believe one of the most helpful things we've done has been to dive deep into some practical legacy work. In 2017, our whole family—myself, NeAnn, NeAnn's mother, Jason, Emily, Cameron, and Jill—went through a series of interviews in order to make written and video recordings our family stories for the next generation. Then, in 2018, my friend Bill High helped us create a family mission and vision statement, along with a set of family values and a stewardship philosophy.

Combined, these efforts have helped provide our family with a unified vision as Jason, Emily, Cameron, and Jill help lead us into the future. The mission and vision statements have given us shared language and goals as we all seek to lead and guide both Jasco and the next generation of Trices. Our hope is that these documents will help us not only pass down our mission and vision as a family, but also emphasize to the next generation the good news of the gospel of Jesus Christ and the importance of discipleship.

The values and stewardship philosophy, meanwhile, have been very important in helping us all get on the same page for the work we do through the Jasco Giving Hope Foundation. As I've already shared, I believe Scripture tells us that the more we give away, the more God gives us *to* give away. While that is an amazing blessing, I'm also aware of the temptation it can pose. I remember sitting down with Jason and Cameron one time and saying, "Guys, the amount of money we've committed to give away this year is enough to buy a private jet. What do you think we should do with it?"

I'll never forget what Jason said. "Dad, please don't tempt us. Give that money away."

I was so thankful for that response. A few years ago, our family began praying about removing that temptation permanently by taking the decision out of our hands. At the time, NeAnn and I owned 84 percent of the business, and Jason and Cameron owned 8 percent each. Since we believe God owns Jasco entirely, we began considering consolidating our ownership into a charitable trust.

The process took several months as we spent lots of time in prayer and discussing the possibility with wise counsel. I studied Scripture on the subject and asked the Lord to put a check in my spirit if it wasn't His will. In the end, we decided to move forward with the plan. NeAnn and I sold our 84 percent to the trust and gave the proceeds of the sale to Giving Hope for further distribution to charities. Jason and Cameron sold their ownership shares to purchase the building and land that Jasco sits on, which we had previously given to Giving Hope, so the proceeds of that sale ultimately went to charitable giving too. They still get their salaries and bonuses for their roles as co-CEOs, and Jasco pays them rent for the property. I draw a salary for my position as chairman of the board. I've long maintained that a company should pay the CEO and chairman salaries and bonuses based on the market price, but who needs more than that? The best thing is to take as much of the balance as you possibly can and use it to spread the gospel of Jesus Christ and facilitate people's discipleship.

The income we would have received from Jasco now goes directly into the trust and facilitates Jasco's operations and provides for tax payments as well as the company's giving. Jason, Cameron, and I are all currently trustees for the trust.

Especially as they near retirement age themselves, Jason and Cameron will need to work to develop a succession plan as I did, whether that ends up being one or more of their children or someone outside the Trice family. We don't know what that plan will be yet, but we trust God to lead the way.

Meanwhile, Jason, Emily, Cameron, Jill, and I now meet monthly with our two Giving Hope employees to discuss where we'll send the money that comes in for foundation. Our mission is to "give to the ministry of Jesus Christ for the purpose of spreading the gospel and equipping the saints to make reproducing disciples." That means that, while we have given to secular nonprofits, especially through our Dollars for Donors and Dollars for Doers employee matching programs, our priority is to give to Christian ministries that focus on evangelism and discipleship, which often includes ministries that have a focus on marketplace, youth, or prison evangelism. We also feel strongly called to give to ministries that promote the Christian education and welfare of children, as well as those that serve the sick, needy, and poor.

In the early days of those monthly meetings, I would take the lead in those discussions since my sons and daughters-in-law were new to the process, but as they've gained experience, I've intentionally stepped back and let them take the lead. They seek God on every decision and have shown great wisdom in finding amazing organizations for us to support. Over the last twenty-eight years, we've been able to support clean-water initiatives in Africa, empower and educate young women in Ghana, assist struggling hospitals during the COVID-19 pandemic, and provide a new building for a day program for adults with developmental disabilities, among many other wonderful outreach and ministry opportunities. I'm confident that the future of Jasco and of the Jasco Giving Hope Foundation is in good hands.

If we count my dad's leadership at Trice Wholesale Electronics where Jasco started as a division, we are already part of that rare 12 percent of family-owned businesses that have successfully transitioned to the third generation. With that in mind, although Jasco is celebrating its fiftieth anniversary in 2025, in many ways we are already a seventy-one-year-old enterprise, since Trice Electronics started in 1954. The care and wisdom Jason and Cameron have shown as they lead Jasco into the future is more than I could have asked for. Together with Emily and Jill, they are keeping the mission of Jasco focused on loving employees well, giving generously, and spreading the gospel. I don't know what the future holds for Jasco, but I'm grateful for all the ways our sons and their families continue the vision. That's all we can do—prayerfully steward what we've been given. Everything else is up to the company's true Owner.

Chapter 10

The Value of Life-Long Discipleship

As Jason and Cameron settled into their leadership roles at Jasco, I found myself with more time on my hands. Finally, I was able to do what I'd wanted to do for so many years: disciple more men. During my years as CEO, I found that I could only disciple two or three men at a time, usually meeting with them early in the morning as Herman and Dan had done with me. And while I'd found great joy and satisfaction in pouring myself into the efforts of doing ministry through Jasco, the Spirit-led desire and call to pursue disciple-making on a deeper level never left me.

Originally, after I became a Christian, the idea of discipling someone else was incredibly intimidating to me. I kept thinking about Jesus's command in Matthew 28:18b-20 (NIV): "All authority in heaven and on earth has been given to me. Therefore go and make disciples of all nations, baptizing them in the name of the Father and of the Son and of the Holy Spirit, and teaching them to obey *everything I have commanded you*. And surely I am with you always, to the very end of the age" (emphasis mine). Trying to teach someone to obey *everything* that Jesus had commanded seemed to require an amazing understanding of Scripture, which I wasn't sure I had. But eventually, the last words of those verses hit home with me: "I am with you always."

Jesus promises to be *with* us in the process. *He* gives us the words to say.

That gave me confidence to begin. A couple of years after becoming a Christian, I reached out to two guys I'd met through CBMC or other business networks and asked if they'd like to begin meeting with me. They agreed, and I began to go through *Operation Timothy* with each of them. Together, we studied and memorized Scripture, shared our struggles, and worked to hold each other accountable. Though I still didn't feel fully confident, most meetings seemed to go well, and I learned to trust Jesus to lead me to the answers He wanted to give to each man's questions. I grew to thoroughly enjoy the friendships that developed out of those meetings, and once Jason and Cameron took over leading Jasco, I was able to slowly increase the number of men I discipled as God brought people across my path. Today, I regularly meet with eleven men.

Finding Freedom from Anxiety
by David Ross,
CEO of TriCorps Security,
discipled by Steve for seventeen years

For two decades, I was a state trooper in Oklahoma. I did all the wild stuff—I was with the tactical team, SWAT team, and the manhunt division, kicking down doors and doing raids and all kinds of things like that. During those years, I don't remember ever being scared. Not once. Looking back, I probably should have been, but I was never anxious or scared at the time.

Twenty-five years ago, I started a corporate security firm here in Oklahoma City. We were one of the first firms of our kind, so we began to grow quickly. And as we grew, I started to worry. The bigger we got, the more anxious I became. I couldn't enjoy the good Lord's blessings because I was worried about losing them. It became debilitating, and I woke up every day in emotional misery.

Just about the time I got to the end of my rope, I was at a Christian gathering of businesspeople, and Steve spoke about his struggle with anxiety and how he overcame it. *That's my story*, I thought. *I've gotta meet this guy and talk to him and figure out how he did it.* As soon as Steve finished speaking, I made a beeline down to the front to shake his hand and tell him how much I appreciated hearing his story. I'm sure he thought I was some kind of maniac. I told him I was struggling with the same thing and would love to buy him lunch sometime and pick his brain.

I had lunch in mind, but Steve had a whole personal relationship in mind called *discipleship*. When we met, he asked me a bunch of questions. Looking back, I can see he was vetting me to make sure I was somebody he could help, but I had no idea what he was doing at the time—I just wanted the magic this guy had found somewhere. A few days later, he called and invited me into a discipling relationship.

I'd been a Christian all my life. I understood what the word *discipleship* meant, but I didn't understand the real depth it could involve. Steve took me under his wing. He said we were going to do four things: meet regularly, study God's Word, be accountable to each other, and memorize Scripture. The first three made sense to me, but I didn't get the value of Scripture memory. You can get the Bible on your phone and just look up a verse. But he was the teacher, and I wasn't going to tell him what to do. So, I went along with it. Now, memorizing Scripture is the most valuable thing anyone has ever taught me. It's hard to articulate the value of having verses in your mind.

As Steve and I got to know each other, it amazed me how similar our stories were. He had some tough times with his parents as a child. I've been there and dealt with similar issues. As he grew his business, he experienced some blessings but also some huge setbacks. Same for me. He had two sons whom he was equipping to take over his business. I have twin sons who are police officers and are set to take over our security firm. It almost seemed like everything this guy had gone through in his life was designed to help me. Specifically, I recall a time I lost a big client, and Steve told me about how Jasco had gotten the General Electric brand. Those kinds of stories made me realize we're not in control of anything. If you have a business, it's not yours. It can go away, or it can flourish, and either of those things are just up to the good Lord. We're just working in it; He's the one in control.

When life knocks you down, it's so good to have a guy you can call. Steve has been that for me. He knows the words to say, and it's not something out of *his* mouth. It's out of the Bible; it's truth. Having somebody like that is invaluable. Like I said earlier, I was at the end of my rope when I met Steve. I don't know what would have happened if we hadn't met, but if it's possible that the worst could have happened, you could say that discipleship saved my life.

In the Old Testament, God used all kinds of things to communicate with His children, from a burning bush in Exodus 3 to a talking donkey in Numbers 22. But after Jesus came to earth, His model shifted, and now He primarily helps His children *through*

> His children. 2 Corinthians 1:3-4 says, "Blessed be the God and Father of our Lord Jesus Christ, the Father of mercies and God of all comfort, who comforts us in all our affliction so that we will be able to comfort those who are in any affliction with the comfort with which we ourselves are comforted by God." God comforts us so that, down the road, we can share that comfort with somebody else. Discipleship is the model God uses to train, educate, and comfort us to help us through hard times.

Jesus' command to teach disciples to obey *all* that He commanded stayed with me, however. There are a lot of commands in those sixty-six books of the Bible, and I soon learned—as I'd noticed for myself with Herman—that it's not possible to teach someone to obey all those commands in only three or four years. We live in a fallen world, and everyone faces new challenges and struggles on a regular basis. If there's not one today, there'll be five tomorrow. As I walked with men through struggles with anxiety, with their marriages or children, with their businesses or health, I was forced to dig deeper into Scripture to find wisdom to share. I learned and grew, and so did they. But like me, I could tell they weren't done learning after only four years. So I continued meeting with them. I now have a couple of guys I've discipled for seventeen or eighteen years, and in the process, I have learned an important principle that I continue to emphasize whenever I talk about discipleship.

True discipleship means walking through life with someone *for* life.

One of the best and most detailed examples of this in Scripture is the relationship between Jesus and the Apostle Peter. In Matthew 4, as Jesus walked along the Sea of Galilee, He saw two brothers, Simon Peter and Andrew, casting their nets into the sea for fish. He said to them, "Follow Me, and I will make you fishers of men" (Matthew 4:19b). They immediately dropped their nets and followed Him. For the next three and a half years, they followed Jesus, watching Him teach and preach, seeing Him come alongside people in their grief and distress, and serving as witnesses to His miracles. Whenever Peter did or said something dumb, Jesus routinely rebuked him and explained God's truth to him. And every time, Peter would repent and grow.

But here's one of the most interesting details to me. After three and a half years, when Jesus was betrayed and taken to court before the Pharisees, what did Peter do? First, he took matters into his own hands and cut off the ear of the high priest's slave (John 18:10). Then he denied even knowing Jesus three times in order to protect himself (John 18:15-27). Even after years of doing life with *Jesus*, the world's best disciple-maker, Peter came up short. Unless we deceive ourselves into thinking we are better than the Apostle Peter, in this life, we will never progress beyond our need to have a mature disciple-maker pour into our lives and hold us accountable.

> **Recovering from Burnout**
> *by Ghena Russu,*
> *Executive Director of Invest Credit,*
> *from Moldova (35 miles from the Ukraine border),*
> *discipled by Steve for seven years*
>
> I met Steve at a business as missions conference in Belfast, Northern Ireland, at the end of a six-month sabbatical I took because of deep burnout from my job. During my sabbatical, I'd spent a lot of time praying and honestly hoping the Lord would show me the

way. But this did not happen. So, when I decided to attend the conference, I remember hoping a solution would be revealed there.

I still vividly remember Steve speaking at the conference. He talked about how he was discipling eleven people, and his goal was to disciple twelve. I thought, *This is probably exactly why I'm here. This is why God took me through all this. He just wants to open a new chapter for me.* After the presentation, I found Steve and told him I needed help figuring out the next stage of my life and seeking the Lord in order to get back to where I was before my burnout.

Because I live in Moldova, Steve was initially hesitant.

"I've never discipled anyone outside my area," he said. "All my meetings are face-to-face."

Steve was also concerned he might have trouble understanding my accent, especially over the phone. But he ended our discussion by saying, "I'll take your card, and I'll pray about it."

About a month later, I contacted him, and he said, "Well, your business card is still on my desk. I've been praying about it, and I'd be willing to give it a try."

It's been about seven years since then, and Steve has played an incredibly powerful role in helping me recover from burnout—not just through his encouragement or prayers, but because he has taught me to memorize Scripture and to continue trusting the Lord with all the challenges in my life. He has often shared his experience with anxiety and depression and how memorizing Scripture has helped him rebound and get back on track. I was not an easy person to deal with, especially when I was at my low point. I argued, I disagreed, I asked questions, and there were moments when I just could not understand some things, but Steve was kind and loving and patient. Today, I'm in a much better place because of his role in my life.

I have learned the power of love, kindness, patience, humility, and vulnerability through the personal example Steve has shown me. He's been very truthful about his own journey and struggles, which has allowed us to develop a very genuine relationship. I've also learned the importance of spiritual disciplines, such as making time to connect with the Lord—to be quiet before Him, and to ask for His guidance and help in each and every area of my life. I will never forget how many times Steve has reminded me that God really cares, that He wants to be present and involved in my life, and that He could turn everything around. Steve also reminds me that the struggles we go through in this life are temporary and light afflictions and we should be more focused on what's to come (2 Corinthians 4:16-18). His goal is not just to help me be better spiritually, but also to help me grow to the point where I'm equipped and capable of discipling other people.

Discipleship is walking with Christ and also with each other. We are not alone, not just because we know that Christ is with us through His Holy Spirit, but also because there are fellow brothers walking alongside us. Discipleship is a relationship of reciprocity, where those who are involved help each other grow and find joy in the relationship. It's living life together—that's what discipleship is all about.

Discipleship also calls for mercy and gently restoring people to a relationship with Jesus. After Jesus's resurrection, Peter returned to fishing—not for men, as he'd been commanded, but for actual fish. Jesus found him out at sea, and, with His help, Peter caught 153 fish (John

21:4-11). Imagine with me, if you will, Peter counting out every one of those fish in the presence of the risen Lord. Then Jesus asked Peter three times if he loved Him. When Peter responded each time in the affirmative, Jesus gave him a command: "Tend My lambs," "Shepherd My sheep," "Tend My sheep" (John 21:15-17).

I believe that we, like Peter, are called by Jesus to shepherd His sheep by walking with a few maturing believers and teaching them the real-life application of God's Word as they go through the trials and tribulations of life. As Jesus questioned and rebuked Peter regarding his blind spots, we are to do likewise for those we disciple, while also allowing them to do the same for us. Finally, we are to equip those we disciple to go out and multiply, finding their own disciples to walk alongside. Discipleship is not a quick and easy process. It requires time and dedication on the part of both the one discipling and the one being discipled. It means walking life together *for* life. But even though it isn't easy, it is well worth the investment.

All Things for Good
by Randall "Randy" Kamp,
CEO of KampCo Foods,
discipled by Steve for seventeen years

Discipleship has influenced me in many ways, but one story that helps illustrate its impact relates to my cancer. In December 2010, I was diagnosed with prostate cancer. I was only fifty years old at the time, so it was a pretty big blow. I called Steve on the day I was diagnosed, and one of the first things he did was to remind me of the message of Romans 8:28, which states: "And we know that God causes all things to work together for good to those who love God, to those who are called according to His purpose." He encouraged me to look for the good that might come out of my cancer diagnosis.

He then recited James 1:2-3 to me: "Consider it all joy, my brethren, when you encounter various trials, knowing that the testing of your faith produces endurance." Both times, I admitted to Steve that, while I knew those verses were true in my head, I didn't yet necessarily believe them in my heart.

In February 2011, I had my prostate removed. Before I was taken back for surgery, several people waited in the pre-op area with me, including my wife, my three daughters, Steve, and four other close friends. As we waited, Steve and the other guys began praying for me.

The surgery went well, and it seemed like there may not be any more issues. About six weeks after the surgery, my daughter mentioned to me that she hoped someday, when she got married, her husband would have godly friends surrounding him during the tough times like my friends had done for me in that hospital room. I immediately thought about my conversation with Steve when I was diagnosed with cancer. I could start to see that some good was coming out of my diagnosis.

That, however, was only the beginning of the story. Although my surgery had gone well, follow-up tests showed the cancer markers rising, so in the summer of 2011, I had thirty-nine radiation treatments. Even after those treatments, the markers still went up.

I went to multiple hospitals looking for answers, and while the markers continued to rise, the doctors could not determine where the cancer was growing. As you can imagine, knowing I still had cancer growing somewhere inside me was stressful at best. I had many conversations with Steve during those years about what the Lord teaches us about hard times. The conversations were not always what I wanted to hear, but they were what I *needed* to hear.

Finally, doctors found a spot they thought might be causing the problem. I had more intense radiation and was put on a new medication. Although the treatment worked in the short term, in early 2022, another test found that the cancer had metastasized and was now in some of my lymph nodes. As a result, my current prognosis is that I will most likely need to be on medication for the rest of my life.

I don't share my story to make anyone feel sorry for me but to outline what I have learned through these trials. Today, I am thankful that I have not had a normal prostate cancer journey, if there is such a thing, because I know that I could not have learned what God wanted me to learn otherwise. Steve and I had many conversations about being thankful for the challenges God has allowed me to have. There are many Scriptures that discuss this, including a few of my current favorites: 1 Peter 4:12-13, 1 Thessalonians 5:18, Ephesians 5:20, and Colossians 3:17. This experience has caused me to trust God more than I ever thought I could, and it has pushed me to make changes in my life that I'm not sure I would have made otherwise. It has encouraged me to put the important things in my life in their proper place.

My cancer journey would have been much harder to navigate without Steve. Steve and I have been walking life together for more than seventeen years now. His accountability and support have been invaluable and have changed my life.

Building Faith Through Developing Spiritual Rhythms

Discipleship is a never-ending learning process. It means becoming a teacher, which in turn means learning faster than your students because of all the prep work you have to do. The men I disciple teach me as much as I teach them. They are always challenging me to dig deeper into Scripture.

There's no one right way to do this. I've personally found *Operation Timothy* to be a good guide to start the process, but there are also many other wonderful discipleship curriculums out there. After more than twenty-five years of discipling men, I've found a few tools and practices especially useful.

First, I always strive to help the guys I disciple get into the habit of hearing, reading, studying, memorizing, meditating on, and applying God's Word to their lives every day, as I learned to do with Dan Williams many years ago.

Second, I emphasize the importance of starting our days with God. As Matthew 6:33 says, "But seek first His kingdom and His righteousness, and all these things will be added to you." And as Paul writes in Ephesians, "For our struggle is not against flesh and blood, but against the rulers, against the powers, against the world forces of this darkness, against the spiritual forces of wickedness in the heavenly places. Therefore, take up the full armor of God, so that you will be able to resist in the evil day, and having done everything, to stand firm" (Ephesians 6:12-13). Having quiet time with God in the morning, before we start our day, is putting on the full armor of God. I often tell the men I meet with that you either put on the full armor of God in the morning, or you walk out the door naked and vulnerable to Satan. I've learned—and I think the guys I've worked with would say the same thing—that the days I don't have my quiet time are much different and more difficult than the days I do.

Third, prayer should always play an important part in that quiet time. For me, because of how many broken marriages I've seen, praying for my marriage is an important part of that. There are several Scripture passages that have become guides for how I pray for my marriage. First, as Paul writes in Ephesians: "Husbands, love your wives, just as Christ also loved the church and gave Himself up for her.... each individual among you also is to love his own wife even as himself, and the wife must see to it that she respects her husband" (Ephesians 5:25, 33b). And then as Jesus says, "Have you not read that He who created them from the beginning made them male and female, and said, 'For this reason a man shall leave his father and mother and be joined to his wife, and the two shall become one flesh'? So they are no longer two, but one flesh. What therefore God has joined together, let no man separate" (Matthew 19:4b-6).

> "Being discipled by Steve set me in a pattern of communing with God every day when I wake up, which has led to a ten-year conversation with God that continues to this day.... There are very few men in my life with whom I have deep conversations or share any problems. Discipleship creates the opportunity for that kind of conversation with someone I trust to provide wise counsel and keep topics private. On the spiritual side, discipleship matters because it helps me stay focused on God in a world that is very chaotic and often ignores that God exists at all. It matters because I know there is always one person in the world who would pick up the phone and help me in a spiritual crisis."
>
> —Scott Klososky,
> Founding Partner of Future Point of View,
> discipled by Steve for seventeen years

This is so countercultural. Instead of marriage being all about you, it's about pouring yourself out for the other person. That certainly didn't describe me in our early marriage. I was so focused on my own needs and the demands of my business that I almost missed out on getting to serve NeAnn and my sons by being a Christ-centered husband and father. I'm still so grateful she hit me over the head with a figurative two-by-four and told me things needed to change. I'm confident that if you follow Jesus's lead and put your family before your work, you can be the right kind of leader in both.

> ### Faithful Followers for Generations to Come
> #### by Reverend Jay R. Smith,
> #### senior pastor at New Covenant Church,
> #### discipled by Steve for seven years
>
> After I graduated from seminary in December 2017, I was looking for ways to continue growing in my faith. I'd been following Jesus for twenty years, since I was sixteen, but I'd always wanted to be more intentional and disciplined in my spiritual practices. Several men from my church suggested that Steve would be a great man to walk alongside me to help me become more intentional with my spiritual disciplines and to hold me accountable in areas of sin and struggle in my life.
>
> Steve and I first met at a local restaurant in Edmond, Oklahoma, sometime in early 2018. I remember feeling incredibly intimidated. I had no idea what to expect and no concept of who Steve was. But those feelings thoroughly washed away after meeting and sharing a

meal with him. He was kind and welcoming, and his accountability in love was precisely what I needed. Additionally, he had the right amount of wisdom and depth to make me appropriately respectful as I prepared for each of our meetings. As we continued to meet, I learned how to prioritize Scripture more deeply in my life, including studying, memorizing, meditating on, and applying the Word of God, and those sinful behaviors that had been common in my life began to have less influence and hold on my life through Steve's accountability.

In hindsight, I've realized how God used those meetings to prepare me for a challenging season. In 2020, I was appointed to be the next senior pastor at the church where I was working. It was a substantial responsibility, and with the pandemic at its earliest stages, there were tremendous difficulties above and beyond the usual leadership challenges. I give all the credit to the work of the Holy Spirit in me and the intentional discipleship process with Steve for keeping me afloat. Those moments of discipleship and training had laid a strong foundation to sustain me in ministry and in life with my family.

These past seven years with Steve have changed my life. Because of this relationship, I am different in every way. I am more committed to daily prayer practices and to studying the Bible. I have won many battles over the flesh and its sinful nature. I am a better leader, pastor, husband, and dad because of the foundation of Jesus in these practices. My formation as a husband and dad is one of the most significant legacies of this intentional discipleship process.

A key conviction that has become integral to my leadership in the local church is the significance of discipleship. For the future of the church, discipleship must be our foundational work. We must

> become more about depth than breadth, and we must devote our lives and time to helping people discover what fully following Jesus means. Our future depends on our commitment to teaching others to follow Jesus as we have been taught and to raise up generations of faithful followers from now until the day Jesus returns.

Today, as I read those passages about marriage, I ask myself: *Do I know how to love NeAnn as Christ loved the church?* I don't think I do, so I have to ask for God's help. Virtually every day, I pray in line with Ephesians 5: "Father, teach me to love NeAnn as Christ loved the church, so that I can pour myself out for her, even to the point of death, and please teach her to love and respect me." NeAnn and I have been married for fifty-three years now, and I believe that prayer has really strengthened our marriage over time. In addition to praying for myself and NeAnn, I pray that same prayer for each of our sons and their wives every morning. Whenever I'm discipling a guy who is struggling in his marriage, I teach him to pray this kind of prayer as well. If every man and every woman in the church would pray like this on a regular basis, how different would marriages be? I don't think we'd have the high divorce rates that we do today. As God's Word tells us in 1 John 5:14-15, "This is the confidence which we have before Him, that, if we ask anything according to His will, He hears us. And if we know that He hears us in whatever we ask, we know that we have the requests which we have asked from Him."

After I pray for Jason's and Cameron's marriages every morning, I turn my focus to the next generation. I pray that my sons and daughters-in-law will train up their children in the way they should go so that when they are old, they will not depart from it (Proverbs 22:6). I pray for the salvation of each of my four grandchildren. Then I pray for each grandchild's future spouse and for their salvation, and finally, I pray that the Lord will raise up nations of reproducing disciples through our family.

"There are some people who come into the world and leave it much better than they found it, and that's Steve. I always joke with Steve that my job in heaven will be pulling weeds in his yard because of how much he's done for me. In the four or five years since we started meeting, I've learned so much from him about depending on God, persevering through challenges, putting obedience in action, and trusting God through everything. Most of all, he's taught me about growing in Christ through Scripture and how to pray for wisdom.

I'm seventy now, and a couple of years ago, I commented to Steve that I wondered if maybe my best days were over.

'Danny,' he said, 'the best days of serving God are always ahead. That's the reason we keep learning and growing.'

Steve is an amazing example of faith in action. He doesn't just talk about his faith—he absolutely lives it. Through both his words and his example, he has taught me that we don't control anything. When we let God drive our lives and trust He knows best, we're able to stop striving and rest."

—DANNY KENNEDY,
MANAGING PRINCIPAL AT WILSHIRE-PENNINGTON GROUP,
DISCIPLED BY STEVE FOR SIX YEARS

I usually end my prayers with something like this: "Father, all that I am is Yours. All that I have is Yours. Please show me this day what You would have me do with the time, with the spiritual gifts, with the talent and the treasure that You have so richly entrusted to me to steward for You." Then, with everything surrendered to Him, I'm able to rest in confidence that it's in His hands, and He is in control. Digging into God's Word, starting the day with a quiet time, and devoting myself to prayer have served me well in my faith over the years. I do my best to teach these practices to the men I disciple, and I pray they will see fruit from them for years to come.

> ### The Smallest Family Will Become a Thousand
> ### by Dr. Richard Kopke,
> ### former CEO of the Hough Ear Institute
> ### and retired ear surgeon,
> ### discipled by Steve for nineteen years
>
> My wife and I have been extremely blessed to have had discipleship relationships with people wherever we have moved throughout twenty-two years of military service, largely through The Navigators. But I have learned so many things through a nearly two-decade friendship and discipleship relationship with Steve Trice.
>
> Through his teaching, and more importantly by his example, I've grown in the practices of daily intake of the Word, prayer, and generous giving of time, talent, and treasure. Steve is a great example of someone who daily hears, reads, studies, memorizes, and meditates on the Word of God. He has faithfully held me accountable on Scripture memory, and I am able to do that now for some of the men I meet with. He has always exemplified being a steady, faithful prayer warrior for my family and me. I am constantly amazed at his daily commitment to pray for us specifically according to our needs. Prayer is hard and time-consuming work, and it is humbling to see the love Steve manifests in wrestling in prayer for us.

Steve has also been a wonderful example of generosity, both with his time and treasure. He has met with me almost weekly since 2006 or so and more often if desired. He served on and chaired the board of our nonprofit, where he continued to share not only his time but his leadership talents. I have also experienced his generosity with his treasure personally when Jasco donated very, very generously to the nonprofit I was blessed to lead.

Being discipled has probably impacted me most in the area of spurring me on in evangelism and helping others practice apprenticeship to Jesus so that multiplication occurs. One of my favorite verses is, "The smallest family will become a thousand people, and the tiniest group will become a mighty nation. At the right time, I, the Lord, will make it happen" (Isaiah 60:22 NLT). Sometimes discipleship involves a short act of obedience, and sometimes it is a process of walking together with Jesus over years.

A few examples come to mind that highlight this point in my mind. I am now a retired ear surgeon, and on one occasion, I received a vision that I interpreted as meaning God wanted me to hold an ear clinic in the Middle East. The short story is that I was able to hold an ear clinic for Syrian refugees in a tent in a refugee camp in Lebanon. God, through friends and family in place there, turned that one clinic into multiple clinics in refugee camps in the region. There were miraculous healings, and a passionate disciple-making woman was raised up by God. Now some fifteen years later, there are five generations of Muslim-background Christian believers in that region and back in Syria.

Another time, I was privileged to disciple a young man for several years who now leads a water provision organization in Africa that emphasizes discipleship. Over the past several years, 20,000 discipleship groups have been started in Zambia through his enterprise. Or, in one final example, my wife and I met a young couple in a Sunday school class for new believers we led when we lived in New York. Lesley, on the first day in class, made this statement, "If someone would just tell me how to become a Christian, I would do it right now." We were able to share and walk with Lesley and her husband in discipleship for about a year. She led her husband, kids, and extended family to the Lord. Now Lesley leads an international ministry that incorporates the Bible into homeschooling throughout the globe.

We took small steps of obedience, others discipled, and God multiplied the smallest family into a thousand people. He did it, but He uses us. What a broad and expansive impact God can have through discipleship.

Discipleship—being apprenticed to Jesus, together with others—is God's plan to reach our world, and I am very privileged that God would call and use me in His great endeavor. Jesus said that He came to give us life and life abundantly (John 10:10). To walk in apprenticeship to Jesus with others is truly living the abundant life. Abundant in deep relationships with our Savior and the saints, and abundant in the joy of seeing someone come to faith, be transformed by the Word and Spirit to be more like the Master, and turn to impact others for eternity. This is great joy indeed!

Loving Your Neighbor—Even Through Difficulties

Several years ago, I started regularly asking the Lord to teach me to love Him with all my heart, soul, mind, and strength, and to teach me to love my neighbor as myself (Mark 12:30-31). I envisioned Him introducing me to the neighbors who lived next door or down the street from me. Instead, over time, he brought three men into my life who faced serious challenges in their lives, including criminal charges, prison sentences, and progressive neurodegenerative disorders.

This was not at all what I'd had in mind when I prayed. Who wants to be a part of situations as complicated as these?

But God had a different plan. I couldn't get away from the truth presented in the story of the Good Samaritan—our neighbors aren't always who we think they'll be and they're not always who we *want* to serve (Luke 10:30-37). Each of these men was essentially lying in the ditch by the side of the road as I walked by, and I felt compelled to do what I could to help them.

That has meant doing what I can to help with any practical needs they have, as well as checking in with them regularly to talk and pray. It's not always easy, and it's certainly not popular—in each of these situations, I'm the only person, or close to the only person, who follows up with these men regularly. Many people tend to back away when life gets messy, but God has continually urged me to keep pressing in.

Jesus never promised discipleship would be easy. It means digging into the messy parts of life and walking side by side through it all. When you walk life for life with another person, trust builds over time, and they'll tell you about everything, including their difficulties, their temptations, and the huge pains they experience in life. Although you can't carry their pain for them—only the Lord can do that—you can walk with them through that pain.

This short life is all about pouring ourselves out for other people. Whether it be our time, talent, treasure, or spiritual gifts, we're called to use all of those and give them away to others. Discipleship has changed my life entirely. It's my privilege to play a small part in walking through the same process with so many others.

Chapter 11

Cultivating a Transformative Culture

As Jasco approaches its fiftieth anniversary, I've been reflecting on how many people it took for us to get to where we are today. The story of Jasco may be the story of a business on one level, but on a much deeper level, it is the story of how God has worked through people to impact so many others around the world. Each of those people who have played a part in Jasco's story are all part of our "cloud of witnesses," if you will, similar to the many heroes of faith described in the book of Hebrews:

> Therefore, since we have so great a cloud of witnesses surrounding us, let us also lay aside every encumbrance and the sin which so easily entangles us, and let us run with endurance the race that is set before us, fixing our eyes on Jesus, the author and perfecter of faith, who for the joy set before Him endured the cross, despising the shame, and has sat down at the right hand of the throne of God (Hebrews 12:1-2).

As my son Jason likes to say, we stand on the shoulders of giants. Jasco is a multigenerational business now, but it has less to do with the multiple generations of Trices and much more to do with the grace of God and the generations of leaders who have built it one brick at a time over the past fifty years.

First and foremost, I always think of my father in that list of giants. For all his struggles as a father to young kids, he was a tremendous businessman who worked hard, cared for his employees, and honored his word with his customers and business partners. Without his generous loan to help me start Jasco as a division of Trice Wholesale Electronics, the company would not exist today.

I mentioned earlier my dad's habit of coming up behind people, slapping them hard on the back, and saying, "Let's roll it!" Those words are written on my dad's tombstone, and our family's use of that phrase has continued through Jason's license plate, which reads, "ROLLINIT." His grandfather said, "Let's roll it," and here we are two generations later "rolling it"—I love the continuation of that legacy.

Another giant in the story of our company is Paul Thompson, who played an important part in Trice Wholesale Electronics' story as well as Jasco's. He started working for my dad in the warehouse around 1955 and then moved on to work for me at Jasco after my dad sold his business around 1984. One day after my dad had passed away, Paul came into my office and propped his feet up on my desk.

"Steve, I need to let you know your dad made me a promise."

"Oh? What did he promise you?" I asked. Dad had been gone for ten years by that point, so I was curious what the mysterious promise could possibly have been.

"He promised he would never make me retire," Paul said. "Down the street from me, a fireman retired, and he came home and died. And up the street from me, a policeman retired, and he came home and died. I don't want that. I want you to carry me out of here feet-first."

I promised him I wouldn't make him retire, and so he continued working in the warehouse for Jasco for another twenty years.

He was always Mr. Congeniality, a delightful guy known for his enthusiasm, big smile, firm handshake, and desire to selflessly serve others. I remember several mornings when I'd arrive at work, go to get something out of my trunk, and suddenly Paul would be there. "I'll get that—I'll carry that for you," he'd say. Any time it snowed, he was out in the parking lot shoveling the sidewalks and helping people into the office. Sometimes when I spoke at company-wide meetings, Paul would come up and take the microphone out of my hand to give his own speech. People always listened intently because Paul had been with Jasco so long, and he was such a great cheerleader for the company. Paul also carried on my dad's tradition of saying, "Let's roll it," to the extent that many people at Jasco now think the phrase came from him.

Paul worked for us until he was ninety-two years old, at which point he had some health issues that led to his retirement in 2005. Between his years at Trice and Jasco, he worked for our family for fifty years.

I remember going to visit Paul at the nursing home where he was living on December 1, 2006. He asked me if I would lend him $300 so he could buy gifts for his family, and he told me this would be his last Christmas on Earth.

"Paul, how do you know this will be your last Christmas on Earth?" I asked.

He looked me in the eye and said, "Steve, you know how I know—Jesus told me," and he pointed to his heart. Paul passed away not quite two months later on January 28, 2007.

To honor his legacy, we named our event center, where we host our monthly company meetings, after him, and we also give away the Paul K. Thompson Award every year at Jasco's Christmas luncheon. It's an award to honor an employee who has demonstrated a heart like Paul's, which is really a heart like Jesus's—someone who seeks to serve and put others first. Employees who win the award then become part of a committee called Paul's Partners, which is entrusted with $100,000 of Jasco's profits each year to give away as they see fit.

In December 2024, Jasco went through what we've termed "The Great Retirement," as a number of long-time employees retired. That included Bill Otte, whom you've heard from already in this book, and Mitch Loukota, whose story you will hear shortly. It also included Donna King, who had worked at Jasco for thirty-six years and led our marketing graphics department most of that time. Known for her artistic abilities, Donna did a beautiful job developing designs for our ads and marketing campaigns as well as the packaging for each of our three thousand products, which is an enormous job, as you can imagine. Both Jason and Cameron reported to Donna when they worked at Jasco during their summers as teenagers, and Cameron jokes that he still worked for her even in his role as CEO.

There are so many others I could name who played critical roles in Jasco's history—Larry Lide, who was our general manager for many years and ran Jasco as CEO for several months; Kent Shiplet, who served as our vice president of marketing for twenty-one years and was there during that critical meeting with Thomson when he told me to take the GE brand; Harold Plunk, our CFO who had a huge impact on our financial ability in our early years and created our all-employee monthly profit sharing incentive program that we still use today; Scott Busby, our CFO who kept us on track financially and was there when we started tithing corporately; Jim Kimball, our COO who came in around the time of our home electrical products (HEP) purchase from GE and discipled Cameron for a number of years; and Dave Hanson, who came to us from GE and helped Jasco succeed with the HEP deal from an engineering and quality-control perspective with our manufacturers in Asia.

I think it's also important to note that although many of the individuals I've mentioned were on the leadership team, those roles are no more important than any other at Jasco. Each of us has a role to play. The executive team may strategize and make high-level plans, but without each team member, our products wouldn't have been created, sold, and shipped, and Jasco wouldn't have been around for very long.

It's hard to pick out individual achievements among our past leaders and employees because we've had such a great team of people over the years. From its conception, Jasco has been very well run—not because of anything I did, but because God sent us the right people to run it.

Nurturing Employee Growth

Thanks to the great people Jasco has been blessed with, we've been able to grow and become a blessing to many through corporate giving, programs for employees, and faith-filled interactions with coworkers. Over the years, so many people have been impacted by the business and the people here. I thank God for those opportunities and for the many ways people who have been influenced can go on to impact others for good too. That's one of the amazing things about cultivating a company culture that focuses on employee growth—it has a multiplying effect, as employees who have experienced life-change go on to influence and work for the good of people within their circles. I'd love to share a few stories with you about ways that God has been transforming and using people within our company.

A Needle in a Haystack
by Mark Schaffner,
Vice President of Efficiency and Product Programs

Before coming to Jasco, I had a long career in consumer electronics. I worked for Thomson Electronics, the company that licensed the GE brand to Jasco, for about seventeen years. Then I ran a surge-protection company in Minneapolis, which was eventually sold to Philips. After that, I became the executive vice president of Bandai's toy division for three years before they made the decision to get rid of that division. Around that time, I got a call from Mitch Loukota, whom I'd worked with during my time at Philips. By this time, Mitch was working for Jasco as their vice president of sales.

"You've been doing some great things in the consumer electronics business for the past twenty years," Mitch said. "Cameron Trice and I were talking—we don't really have a power division, but Cameron's looking for a power guy for our new VP of product development."

"Well, I'm a power guy," I said. "What you're looking for is a needle in a haystack, but I'm probably that needle."

In addition to the job being the right fit, my son had married a woman from Tulsa, Oklahoma, and started a family there. Family has always been my number-one priority, so even though my wife and I weren't initially sure about living in Oklahoma, we were excited to be closer to our son's family.

Every time I tell this story, the hair on the back of my neck goes up because when does this kind of thing ever happen? What are the odds of finding a power guy who's been in the consumer electronics business for a long time? There are not that many of us. And the fact that I was this guy from New Jersey who didn't even know where Oklahoma City was at the time but had family in Oklahoma—how does that happen? It was like *divine intervention*. Having all those touchpoints come together must make you think there is a purpose and a true guiding light. That is something that I feel deep in my heart. Without that guidance and that guiding light, these things don't just happen. Jasco has been my home for over a decade, and I'm so grateful to Steve for giving me this opportunity to work and to be a member of the Jasco family.

Drawn by Generosity
by Celena McCord,
Director of Generosity

I actually came to Jasco because of their generosity. During COVID, I was working for a hospital in Oklahoma City, and Jasco pledged a million dollars to support organizations that were on the front lines of COVID relief. Our hospital was the recipient of one of those gifts and was able to buy much-needed ventilators for the increased number of patients with respiratory issues due to COVID. And then Jasco just kept showing up. They brought PPE [personal protective equipment], they brought face masks—they kind of just kept checking in. "How are you?" "Are you guys doing okay?" "What do you need?" So, when I saw the opportunity to work at Jasco and be part of Giving Hope, I remembered their generosity during COVID and thought, *That's something I'd love to be a part of.*

An Answer to Prayer
by Jeff Cato,
Vice President of Marketing and E-Commerce

Around the time I was considering a career change, my wife said to me, "You know, babe, if there were one company I could see you really enjoying working for, it would be Jasco." I had to agree. Jasco has a great reputation in the Oklahoma City community. Anybody who talks about Jasco and the Trice family never has anything bad to say about them. Then, around that time, I met Cameron Trice and had the opportunity to apply for a job at Jasco. My wife feels like my job was an answer to prayer, and I do too. With the way timing and the details fell into place, it feels like a real God story that I'm even here. I truly believe God has protected this company because of the way the Trice family has been obedient to the things they're supposed to do. They're not perfect people, but they are people after God's own heart.

Thanking God for Challenges
by Mitch Loukota,
Executive Vice President of Sales

I've always tried to make sure I have a good relationship with Steve, so every year or so, I would invite him to lunch. No agenda really, just a desire to talk. On one occasion eight or nine years ago, there was a really challenging situation with one of our retailers. I won't go into all the details, but it was just going wrong in every way. Every single day, I would have a meeting with our product team at 7:30 in the morning to get an update and try to manage the situation.

As I headed to lunch with Steve, I kept thinking, *Don't talk about that. That's not something good to talk about. Talk about other things.* As you might imagine, of course it came up because it was all I was thinking about anyway. Steve asked me a couple of clarifying questions and then said, "Mitch, is this a work problem, or is this a spiritual problem?"

I sat there and considered his question. I knew he wanted me to say it was a spiritual problem, but I couldn't see how this issue I was struggling with was a spiritual problem.

"It's a work problem, Steve," I said. "This is not a spiritual problem."

"I just want to challenge you in that," he replied. "You've told me that you're waking up in the middle of the night, and it's causing you a lot of stress. You are fearful for the future if you don't solve this." He started telling me some stories from his life about similarly challenging situations.

"Have you thanked God for this problem?" he asked.

I have to laugh as I remember my response.

"No, I haven't thanked God for this," I said. "I don't want this."

But Steve just sees things differently. In that one moment, he was discipling me and challenging me to think differently too. That kind of care and mentoring seeps out of him all the time. That memory is so poignant because there I was with this huge issue and I had the CEO of the company telling me to thank God for it. Do my best and let God take care of the rest. I walked away from that conversation thinking how wise his advice had been.

Now, several years later, I've gotten super comfortable "considering it all joy" (James 1:2). I have even been able to pray a prayer of thanksgiving for problems that I am facing. I know that, in the future, problems will get resolved because God's going to resolve them all, so I can consider it joy. I can have confidence that it's all going to be okay. I think that's probably the best thing that Steve does—he always brings us back to the fact that God is in control. And his sons do it too. They constantly remind us that no matter what happens, even if we lose it all, God is in control and our perspective of the world doesn't change. We're not going to lose our joy or our hope or our confidence due to things that happen here on earth. It's so comforting to live my life this way.

A Rich Experience
by Preston Nuckols, Associate Product Manager

One time, Jasco hosted a Weight Watchers class. I thought, *Well, I'm doing okay, but I'm going to go to the class and see if I can learn a little bit.* The class revealed to me that I was out of shape, so I followed the program, dropped forty pounds, and started cycling and running. Now I've completed an Iron Man Triathlon. I've also done seventeen other triathlons and more than ten marathons. And it's all because of this company.

Another time, Jasco hosted Financial Peace University, a course from Dave Ramsey. At that time, I was in debt, and I didn't have a clue how to manage my money. I thought I did—I thought I should go buy stocks or something—but I didn't have a clue. I didn't even have a retirement plan. I took the course fifteen years ago, and today, I'm completely out of debt. My house is paid for. My car is paid for. I am financially wealthy because of that. It's because of Jasco and the courses they offer to their employees. They focus on the well-being of their employees and give us resources and tools to grow as individuals.

I now have a "random acts of kindness" line item in my budget. I put fifty or a hundred bucks in that little account, and when I go to the store, I'll sometimes pay for my drink and say, "Just get the guy behind me too." It's always a really positive experience. The thing is, Jason and Cameron taught me to do that. Their example made that change in my life. Today, I enjoy finding ways to help other people because Jasco has set that example for me and for all their employees.

As the 2007 recipient of the Paul K. Thompson Award, I get to be part of Paul's Partners, which really gives me something to live up to. I feel really honored to be able to help people. I don't have that much money to give away on my own, but through Paul's Partners, I'm able to give significant gifts—tens of thousands of dollars—to help people, and I think that encourages me to want to be a better person.

That's the heart of this company. You peel back the money and the marketing and you get into that good, rich soil of how they're developing people. Jasco's leadership team is developing team members' souls so that we can be better people and learn to care for and love others. As a company, Jasco is setting that example for their employees, and a lot of us are learning from that example.

> We're finding a rich experience by giving generously and getting involved in a mission that is bigger than ourselves.

Each individual mentioned in this chapter—and many, many more—is a part of the story God has woven through Jasco's history. It has taken so many people over the past fifty years to build Jasco into the business and ministry that it is today, and it is a great honor to be a part of something that has become so much bigger than me or my family. As Jasco's cloud of witnesses—both those involved in the company and those impacted by it in some way—continues to grow, I pray we will focus on running the race marked out for us, as Hebrews 12 says. Whether the road ahead is smooth and easy or marked by treacherous terrain, keeping our eyes on Jesus is the best way to continue the legacy we've built together.

Chapter 12

Three Keys to Endurance

The year 2020 could have easily been considered both the best of times and the worst of times for both Jasco and my family. The COVID-19 pandemic raced its way across the globe, resulting in lockdowns and a worldwide medical crisis. But because people across the nation suddenly needed to set up home offices for remote work, the demand for the types of consumer electronics and power products that Jasco sells shot through the roof. Jasco's business hit an all-time record in profit and in products sold that year. On the surface, the business was on top of the world as we approached Christmas that year.

Yet behind the scenes, things were much tougher. All year long, the entire Jasco team worked tirelessly to meet the increased demand, often dealing with angry customers when we couldn't provide supply fast enough due to the strain on our employees and global supply chain disruptions. Toward the end of 2020, Jason and Cameron hit one of their rare seasons when they disagreed on how to move forward with a certain aspect of the business, and the three of us were working together to find a solution.

And then, on December 19, 2020, I began struggling to breathe.

Cameron drove me to the emergency room, with both of us expecting I'd be able to come home later that day. Instead, I was admitted to the

ICU after being diagnosed with COVID. My oxygen saturation had dropped extremely low, and I wasn't sure what the outcome would be.

Due to the hospital's COVID restrictions, my family wasn't allowed to visit me. I was alone in the ICU, surrounded by people on ventilators, many of whom were dying. During my second night in the hospital, I looked up at the ceiling and said, "Well, Father, is this it?"

Immediately, Philippians 1:23-26 came into my mind: "But I am hard-pressed from both directions, having the desire to depart and be with Christ, for that is very much better; *yet to remain on in the flesh is more necessary for your sake*. Convinced of this, I know that I will remain and continue with you all for your progress and joy in the faith, so that your proud confidence in me may abound in Christ Jesus through my coming to you again" (emphasis mine).

Right then I knew: I wasn't going anywhere. I was going to get well.

And I did, but the journey was a long one. I had many days ahead when I was concerned again about whether I would survive, especially during the next nine days in the ICU where people were dying from COVID every day. For my part, I developed double pneumonia, which gave me congestive heart failure. Though I eventually recovered, today I have only 60 percent lung capacity, a pacemaker, erratic low blood pressure issues, and occasional atrial fibrillation (A-fib), which recently required me to undergo an outpatient cardioversion procedure. I take steroids regularly to keep my blood pressure from dropping because my adrenal glands no longer function properly, and I'm on blood thinners to avoid blood clots and a consequential stroke that could result from my A-fib.

Throughout my time in the hospital, and especially during those early days in ICU, I called my family as often as I could to tell them I loved them and to say some of the things I wanted to be sure they knew if the worst should happen. I wasn't allowed to have visitors the entire time I was admitted due to the COVID protocols in place at that point. Thank God for FaceTime. Here's how Cameron remembers those long weeks:

> I remember talking to Dad on the phone a couple of times, and he started talking about some legacy things, and it was like we were almost having a deathbed conversation. I'd say, "Dad, come on, what are we doing? Let's get you out of there. You'll be out in a week." But at that point, we all knew there was a possibility he wouldn't make it. I mean, there were people dying left and right all around us. I had some really dark days when I thought my dad might not make it. The end of 2020 was the best time in our company's history financially, but between the disconnect with my brother and my dad getting COVID, those were also some of the worst months of my life.
>
> When Dad emerged from all of that, every year that goes by and every year I get to celebrate Christmas with him feels like a bonus year. What a blessing.

After forty-four days in the hospital, I was finally released on February 1, 2021. I still had a long recovery ahead of me as I was on oxygen and spent most of my time resting in bed or a recliner. My bride, NeAnn, was a terrific caregiver through all of that.

Despite all the health struggles, including the ones that are ongoing, I'm alive, and I'm so grateful for that.

Lessons from Fifty Years in Business

For Jasco, business took a sharp turn downward in 2021. Thinking the red-hot demand of 2020 would continue, the company bought a ton of extra inventory, but then demand dried up. By the end of 2022, Jasco had racked up $50 million in excess and idle inventory and $110 million in new debt. Since 95 percent of our manufacturing was done in China, we'd also been hit hard by the 25 percent tariffs imposed by President Donald Trump a few years earlier, and we had to work toward developing new manufacturing relationships in Vietnam, Cambodia, Thailand, and the Philippines. All those struggles meant that in 2022, for the first time since 2008, we had to lower our corporate giving from 50 percent to 15 percent. From the beginning, we've tried to limit our giving to no more than 30 percent of a nonprofit's budget to keep them from becoming entirely reliant on us in case something happens to the business. But this was still an extremely tough decision for us to make.

If there's one lesson I've learned in my almost forty years as Jasco's CEO—one that I think Jason and Cameron are learning now as well—it's this: God is sovereign. He is in total control, in both good times and bad. I saw that in 1996 when Jasco almost lost all of Target's business and came out on the other side with the GE brand, in 2004 when we bought the HEP business from GE, and in 2008 when we doubled our giving and watched God provide. And now, in their roles as co-CEOs, Jason and Cameron have been watching God do the same kind of thing for the past four years.

Over the past fifty years, Jasco's leadership team and I have found three primary keys to moving through difficult times as a company: prayer, adaptability, and perspective.

First, I can't overemphasize the importance of surrendering everything to God in prayer. We rarely, if ever, have the answers to our own problems, but God does. He knows exactly what to do. As a result, whenever challenging situations arise, I've learned to pray: *Father, thank You for the lessons You're teaching us. What would You have us do with*

Your company, Jasco, that's now in this difficult position? Put on our hearts what You'd have us change.

I've shared in earlier chapters about how my struggles with anxiety and depression began to fade as I immersed myself in Scripture and discipleship. Prayer also played a huge role in this. As I've mentioned before, through studying Scripture with Herman and Dan, my life verse became Philippians 4:6-7: "Be anxious for nothing, but in everything by prayer and supplication with thanksgiving let your requests be made known to God. And the peace of God, which surpasses all comprehension, will guard your hearts and your minds in Christ Jesus."

The truth found in these words helped me develop a regular practice of surrendering my anxious thoughts to the Lord. Every time an anxious thought appears, I pray, *Father, forgive me for my anxiety. Strengthen me. Thank You for the circumstance that is causing me to have these thoughts. Teach me everything You want me to learn from this circumstance. I cast all my anxiety on You and give all of it to You. Thank You, thank You, thank You for everything that You're teaching me, and help me to trust You with all these circumstances.*

Just as Philippians 4:7 promises, praying in this manner completely relieves me of my fears, as God's peace comes to guard my heart and mind in Christ Jesus.

As I mentioned briefly in a previous chapter, I've discovered over time that generosity has also had a huge impact on my anxiety. I used to idolize money—it was all about me and how much I could make. But as I grew in my relationship with God, began giving more money away, and discovered how God always gave me more in return so that I could continue to give even more away, I was able to let go of the desire for more money. I began to trust Him completely instead of worrying about what the future might bring.

Today, even in the midst of troubling times in my own life, at Jasco, or in our country, my anxiety issues are very quick and very light. I don't worry about things anymore because God is in control over it all.

Second, adaptability is vital for any business. One recent change for Jasco has been to increase our investment in digital marketing. This both supports the major retailers we sell to and recognizes that since the majority of consumers now shop online, we can maximize sales through our website by finding influencers to promote our products. Instead of only selling to brick-and-mortar businesses, we now have a digital-first marketing focus and sell directly to consumers.

I love what Jason had to say about Jasco's willingness to adapt throughout its fifty years in existence:

> We've adapted a ton as a company over the years, from starting out selling accessories for CB radios, then adding accessories for audio, video, computers, and telephones, to now selling LED lighting and smart home lighting controls. Technology has evolved a lot over the last fifty years, and we've evolved and innovated with that. We started out manufacturing in Japan, then moved to Taiwan and China, and now we have moved mostly to other Asian countries like Vietnam and Cambodia. When I worked in the warehouse as a teenager, we packaged most of the products in-house, but now we've outsourced the packaging to the same factories that do our manufacturing. For a long time we were a company that sourced and sold products, but now we also develop and invent patentable products that are truly unique compared to other offerings on the market today.

I like the Margaret Mead quote that says, "Never doubt that a small group of thoughtful, committed citizens can change the world. Indeed, it is the only thing that ever has." That's exactly what Jasco has done over the years. We've got people who put God first and show up, work hard, and solve one problem at a time as they go. And we've been pretty successful because of that. We've survived and thrived.

Finally, perspective can also play a huge part in a business's ability to move through challenges. In our annual company-wide meeting in 2024, Cameron talked about this point, encouraging our employees to consider the wisdom of Philippians 4:8, which says, "Finally, brethren, whatever is true, whatever is honorable, whatever is right, whatever is pure, whatever is lovely, whatever is of good repute, if there is any excellence and if anything worthy of praise, dwell on these things." He went on to challenge our team to take a wider perspective and not get sucked into a negative way of thinking. I'd love to share a few of Cameron's words with you:

We live in a society bent on nursing old wounds and highlighting what is wrong with just about everything. I can make the case that, objectively, these are the best of times, but, subjectively—the way we see it—our world is in the worst of times. And that's a sad thing. The facts haven't changed, but the way we view them is very different. We've grown accustomed to seeing our world, our lives, and ourselves through a lens of negativity.

Here are a couple examples of what I'm talking about. Sound bite: Crime is the worst it's ever been. Fact: According to the Bureau of Justice Statistics, US violent crime and property crime rates each fell 71 percent between 1993 and 2022.[1] Sound bite: Inflation is the worst it's ever been. Fact: When Jimmy Carter was president, he inherited massive inflation from Ford, and in 1980, inflation hit a record high of 14.6 percent, which is more than double the highest inflation rate in the last couple of years.[2] In the US, we have electricity, indoor plumbing, running water—all these things that a lot of people in this country didn't have fifty or sixty years ago, and that a lot of people worldwide still don't have today.

Or let's talk about Jasco. We're on our third year of declining sales. That's one perspective. But did you know that Jasco is still ten times as large as it was in 2000? We're wildly more diversified by customer since we're no longer dependent on Target as we were for decades. We now sell millions upon millions of products through every mass merchandiser and major online retailer, accounting for over 87,000 retail locations. Our manufacturing is likewise diversified by country of origin since we're no longer dependent on China for all of our supply, and we are diversified by brand because we're no longer significantly dependent on GE. Amazing things are happening, even though we've been pruned to some degree.

When you consider the things in this world, I would really encourage you to be grateful for all the good things. If you harbor the negative, that's where your mindset goes, and you're more likely to reflect that darkness. Whereas if you harbor the light and focus on the good things and see the joy in the world, the light that I see as the light of Christ comes out of you and is put on a hill, as the Bible says in Matthew 5:16, for people to see and be influenced by positivity.

Stewarding Healthy Roots

When I look at what our sons and their executive team have gone through in the past few years, I think they've done an outstanding job. They've prayerfully worked through the principles of prayer, adaptability, and perspective as described above, and they've innovated and found ways to reduce excess inventory and debt. Today, Jasco is debt free again and in a good position to begin to grow once more.

Jason, Cameron, and I often envision Jasco as a tree. There are times when we are going to be pruned, but as Jason often says, pruning is a godly process, as God cuts back what is no longer needed so that we can produce more fruit (John 15:2). The tree may look smaller afterward than it once did, but our job as leaders is to do what we can to make sure the roots and the trunk of the tree stay strong and healthy so that it can continue producing fruit for future generations. Jason describes it this way: "Sometimes protecting the tree requires leaders to make tough decisions, but we're trying to emulate the gentleness and love of our God in the business decisions we make, even in hard times. We give God all the glory for the good times, and we trust Him in the tougher times."

We have no doubt that more tough times are ahead, but we are hopeful about the future God has for this company. As Cameron said in his presentation in the 2024 company meeting:

> We're going to grow back. And we're going to have to adapt and evolve as different headwinds hit us, but every time we adapt, new branches spring out, and we become stronger and more diverse as a company. That's what it's all about. It's about the longevity. It's about us playing the long game and surviving and thriving and bringing the next generation some of the success we've had over the years and being able to continue to give and be incredibly charitable and generous in all the things that we do.

As Jasco approaches its fiftieth anniversary in the summer of 2025, we are incredibly blessed to still be here. The Jasco team has survived many difficult times in the past half-century, but through it all, we have found ways to grow as individuals, thrive as a business, and impact thousands if not millions of lives along the way. We have been pruned time and time again, but—all thanks be to God—the roots are still healthy, and so the fruit continues to grow.

Conclusion

Last winter, our whole family gathered for my mother-in-law's ninety-seventh birthday. A few days afterward, one of my half-sisters texted me. I responded and sent her a picture of our family we'd taken at Fran's celebration.

"Wow, what a beautiful family," she wrote in reply.

The very fact I have such a beautiful family today is miraculous to me. Statistically, because my parents divorced and then remarried other people, I was significantly more likely to get divorced myself (perhaps as much as 50 to 90 percent more likely) than a child of parents who stayed together.[1] As a child of alcoholics, I was four times more likely to become an alcoholic myself.[2] I also had an increased risk for anxiety and depression.[3]

Yet here I am at seventy-seven years old with a strong and happy marriage that has lasted fifty-three years and counting, two sons who have each been happily married for close to twenty-five years, and four wonderful grandchildren. I'm free from addiction, and though anxiety can sometimes still be a struggle, my troubles with it are light and momentary compared to what I once experienced. I'm also, through our Lord, the very thankful founder of an incredible fifty-year-old business that continues to impact people for Christ every day all around the world.

And this is all thanks to Jesus and the strength He produced in me through the power of one-on-one discipleship.

As I think back on my early life and picture that little boy sitting alone on the front porch steps waiting for his dad to arrive, I'm filled with compassion for him. If I could, I'd tell him that sometimes people make decisions that can make life very difficult. This fallen world is full of pain and sorrow. And, without God, life is exponentially harder.

However, when we surrender our lives to follow Jesus, God promises to be with us, always. He is the Father who will always come for us.

I believe God sent each of us to this world for what is, in the scope of eternity, a very short one-hundred-year school, give or take a few years. Every day, we have the opportunity to learn something new, both from God and from other people, as He teaches us and prepares us for eternity. Sometimes those lessons are full of joy, and sometimes they are very painful, but even in the middle of the most difficult lessons, God is present. He's able to take complete care of us. We just have to learn to look to and trust in Him.

When we do, He opens the door for us, like my mom opened the door that night as I waited on the porch. God sees us sitting alone in our pain, and He calls out to us.

"Come on in, son," He says. "It's time to rest."

> *"Come to Me, all who are weary and heavy-laden,*
> *and I will give you rest.*
> *Take My yoke upon you and learn from Me,*
> *for I am gentle and humble in heart,*
> *and you will find rest for your souls."*
> —Matthew 11:28-29

Next Steps: Invest in Your Family's Future

This book is a ministry of Legacy Stone Publishing, the nonprofit arm of Legacy Stone. Legacy Stone exists to raise up multigenerational families who live according to biblical purpose and impact culture positively for years to come. If you are looking to invest in the future of your family, Legacy Stone offers the following ways to help you build a strong family based on biblical principles:

Explore the Family Resource Center: Find resources to help you build a solid foundation for your family. Browse articles covering a wide range of topics, such as how to navigate conflict, effective communication strategies, and understanding different personality types.

Connect Your Church: Introduce your church or community group to Legacy Stone's small group curriculum that equips families to thrive and learn how to create a lasting vision, write a family mission statement, and determine guiding values together.

Create a Plan: Use Legacy Stone's *7 Generation Family Legacy* study to equip your family and others in your community with a roadmap for biblical, generational success. This study will help you identify what you can do today to help your family walk in its biblical purpose for the next seven generations and beyond.

Visit legacystone.com to learn more about these resources and to get started for free with Legacy Stone's three-part course, *Winning as a Family*.

Acknowledgments

Though writing this book was a wonderful journey, I never could have done it without the encouragement and assistance of some wonderful people who selflessly poured themselves out for me—in some cases, for the past several decades. I want to give a heartfelt thanks to the following people.

First and foremost, to the love of my life, my bride of now fifty-three years, NeAnn, who has walked my challenging life with me through thick and thin. Through all my struggles she has been there to encourage and assist me in my every need, all while nurturing and raising our two wonderful sons.

To Dr. Herman Reece and Dan Williams, who met with me individually every week for four and twelve years, respectively. Though Herman is now home with our Lord, Dan still meets with me monthly. These men walked life with me and taught me to hear, read, study, memorize, meditate on, and apply God's Word to my life daily, which completely transformed the way I think (Romans 12:2). In turn, their teaching and encouragement has led me to help others.

To our sons, Jason and Cameron, two highly intelligent men who both went away to universities in other states and found good jobs in those distant locations after graduation, but eventually came home to reunite our growing family and help grow our wonderful three-generation business.

To our wonderful grandchildren, Ainsley, Landon, Connor, and Spencer, who are all either attending or will soon attend college before determining whether they may be called to participate in and extend the legacy of our family-stewarded business.

To David Green, founder and CEO of Hobby Lobby, for writing the foreword and for his example to us for so many years on how to steward a successful business for our Lord.

To Bill High, who guided our family in how to build a biblical family legacy, regularly encouraged me to write this book, and provided great insight into the book's content, design, and formatting.

To Ruthie Burrell, who tirelessly interviewed me and several others, and drafted and coordinated every facet of this book's creation.

About the Author

Steve Trice is the founder of the Jasco Products Company, a business that designs and distributes over 3,000 consumer electronic and electrical products through over 87,000 retail locations under Jasco's own brands and brands they license, including GE, Philips, Disney, Energizer, and more. For the past fifty years, Steve has led Jasco to deliver excellent products, empower its employees, and impact its community. Steve's sons, Jason and Cameron, became co-CEOs of Jasco in 2014 as Steve transitioned to chairman of the board. Jason and Cameron continue to steward the company's vision into the future. Steve and his family live in Oklahoma City.

Endnotes

Chapter 1: The Seeds of a Scarcity Mentality

1. Clayton Buck, Paul Hemez, and Lydia Anderson, "How Does Your State Compare With National Marriage and Divorce Trends?" United States Census Bureau, October 8, 2024, https://www.census.gov/library/stories/2024/10/marriage-and-divorce.html.

2. "A Short Narrative History of PMA," PoncaMilitaryAcademy.com, accessed January 21, 2025, http://poncamilitaryacademy.com/picture_library/PMA%20History.pdf.

Chapter 2: New Struggles, Old Patterns

1. Miller-Jackson's old building can still be visited in the Bricktown area of Oklahoma City today.

2. Brian Will, "Why Do So Many Business Startups Fail? Ways to Set Yourself Up for Success," *Forbes*, February 10, 2023, https://www.forbes.com/councils/forbesbusinesscouncil/2023/02/10/why-do-so-many-business-startups-fail-ways-to-set-yourself-up-for-success.

Chapter 4: The Problem with Self-Sufficiency

1. Sonya Colberg, "Edmond Chiropractor who received new hands dies at age 60," *The Oklahoman*, August 21, 2015, https://www.oklahoman.com/story/lifestyle/health-fitness/2015/08/21/edmond-chiropractor-who-received-new-hands-dies-at-age-60/60728439007.

2. Steve Trice with Phil Downer, *A Friend Under Fire: "But No One Knew," Discipling a Friend to Safety and Fulfillment*, CBMC, Inc., 2016.

3. "Suicide Data and Statistics," U.S. Centers for Disease Control and Prevention, March 26, 2025, https://www.cdc.gov/suicide/facts/data.html.

4. See Adam England, "Why the Men's Suicide Rate Is So High," Healthline Media, August 4, 2023, https://www.healthline.com/health/mens-health/mens-suicide-rate; Helene Schumacher, "Why more men than women die by suicide," *BBC*, March 17, 2019, https://www.bbc.com/future/article/20190313-why-more-men-kill-themselves-than-women; and "Why are suicide rates so high amongst men?" *Priory Group*, accessed January 24, 2025, https://www.priorygroup.com/blog/why-are-suicides-so-high-amongst-men.

Chapter 5: God's Model for Life Change

1. Janelle Ash, "Kate Middleton helps teen with cancer fulfill 'bucket list' dream after finishing her own chemotherapy treatment," *Fox News*, October 2, 2024, https://www.foxnews.com/entertainment/kate-middleton-helps-teen-cancer-fulfill-bucket-list-dream-after-finishing-own-chemotherapy-treatment.

2. "Medical team helps cancer patient make ambitious trek to Mount Everest," *Synthesis*, summer 2024, https://health.ucdavis.edu/synthesis/issues/summer2024/compassionate-care/medical-team.html.

3. Rebecca O'Neill, "Cancer patient, 82, sets sail on 20,000-mile voyage," *BBC*, June 18, 2024, https://www.bbc.com/news/articles/cydd1lq446mo.

4. Karina Bland, "Women Who Inspire: Hayley Arceneaux," *St. Jude Inspire*, March 8, 2024, https://www.stjude.org/inspire/series/possibilities/women-who-inspire-hayley-arceneaux.html.

5. See Matthew 4:19, 9:9, 19:21; Mark 1:17, 8:34; Luke 5:27, 9:59; John 1:43, 12:26.

6. This phrasing is adapted from the Navigators' Word Hand Illustration. For more information, see "The Word Hand Illustration," The Navigators, accessed February 28, 2025, https://www.navigators.org/resource/the-word-hand.

7. "Operation Timothy," *CBMC Heartland*, accessed February 28, 2025, https://heartland.cbmc.com/Operation-Timothy.

Chapter 6: The Surprising Path of Stewardship

1. "George Müller on God's Guidance," GeorgeMuller.org, accessed February 28, 2025, https://www.georgemuller.org/devotional/the-life-of-george-muller.

Chapter 7: You Can't Outgive God

1. Water4, accessed June 5, 2025, https://www.water4.org.

2. "Mission and Ministry," Light Christian Academy, accessed March 6, 2025, https://www.lightchristian.academy/mission.

Chapter 8: Entrusting Your Family to God

1. This saying is frequently attributed to financial analyst Dan Peña.

Chapter 9: Nurturing Next-Gen Leaders

1. "Family Business Facts," Cornell: SC Johnson College of Business, accessed February 17, 2025, https://business.cornell.edu/centers/smith/resources/family-business-facts.

2. "Family Business Facts," Conway Center for Family Business, accessed February 19, 2025, https://www.familybusinesscenter.com/resources/family-business-facts.

Chapter 12: Three Keys to Endurance

1. John Gramlich, "What the data says about crime in the U.S.," Pew Research Center, April 24, 2024, https://www.pewresearch.org/short-reads/2024/04/24/what-the-data-says-about-crime-in-the-us.

2. Scott Horsley, "This is what was happening 40 years ago, the last time inflation was this high," NPR, February 13, 2022, https://www.npr.org/2022/02/13/1080464204/this-is-what-was-happening-40-years-ago-the-last-time-inflation-was-this-high.

Conclusion

1. "Divorce Statistics: Over 115 Studies, Facts and Rates for 2024," Wilkinson & Finkbeiner, accessed February 18, 2025, https://www.wf-lawyers.com/divorce-statistics-and-facts.

2. "Alcohol Use in Families," *American Academy of Child & Adolescent Psychiatry*, No. 17, updated May 2019, https://www.aacap.org/AACAP/Families_and_Youth/Facts_for_Families/FFF-Guide/Children-Of-Alcoholics-017.aspx.

3. Stacy Mosel, L.M.S.W., edited by Linda Armstrong, "Children of Alcoholics: Growing Up with an Alcoholic Parent," June 18, 2024, https://americanaddictioncenters.org/alcohol/support-recovery/child.

www.ingramcontent.com/pod-product-compliance
Lightning Source LLC
Chambersburg PA
CBHW012007120526
44580CB00018B/137/J